Laws Governing Energy Medicine Practitioners

Laws Governing Energy Medicine Practitioners

LINNIE THOMAS

Laws Governing Energy Medicine Practitioners © 2015 by Linnie Thomas. All rights reserved. No part of this publication may be used or reproduced in any manner whatsoever without written permission, except in the case of brief quotations embodied in critical articles and reviews. For further information, please contact the publisher.

Published by Ellinwood Publishing

Library of Congress Cataloging-in-Publication Data

Thomas, Linnie, 1946 –

Laws governing energy medicine practitioners/Linnie Thomas,

ISBN-13: 9781522797807
ISBN-10: 1522797807

   1. Laws – energy medicine. I. Title.

Printed in the United States of America
First Printing

7 6 5 4 3 2 1

Legal Disclaimer:
This publication is designed to provide accurate and authoritative in formation in regard to the subject matter covered. It is sold with the understanding that neither the author nor the publisher is engaged in the provision or practice of law or medical, nursing, massage, or professional healthcare advice or services in any jurisdiction. If legal advice or other professional assistance is required, the services of a qualified legal professional should be sought. Neither CreateSpace nor the author is responsible or liable, directly or indirectly, for any form of damages whatsoever resulting from the use (or misuse) of information contained in or implied by these documents.

Dedicated to
All Energy Medicine Practitioners
And especially
to
Dawn Warnaca

Acknowledgments

I wish to thank the following people:

Susan Holtorf for her time spent editing this book, and her excellent suggestions for changes.

Dawn Warnaca for her encouragement and support for this project.

Kathy Moreland for her contribution concerning Canadian laws.

Lisa Gordon for suggesting I write the book.

Cynthia Hutchison for her belief in me.

Susan Kiley for teaching me what it means to be a professional.

Leslie Gifford for all the times she picked me up when I was down, and for her constant and abiding support.

Barbara Dahl for teaching me Healing Touch

All the wonderful clerks at the various state departments for steering me in the right direction for legal information.

Introduction

Reasons for this book

A few years ago one of my mentees advertised her Healing Touch services on Craig's List. About a week later she received notification to appear in front of the Oregon Massage Board and that she was facing a possible six thousand dollar fine.

Some of the requirements for certification with Healing Touch Program include documenting one hundred healing sessions and spending a minimum of one year with a mentor, which is where I came into the picture.

My mentee had failed to mention in her ad, that she was a Healing Touch Program apprentice, and that she would be doing energy work. Many years ago a group of prostitutes came up from Nevada advertising their services as "healing touch". The Oregon Board of Massage keeps a sharp eye out for this kind of thing. They thought that my mentee was either practicing massage illegally, or advertising for lady-of-the-evening services. Once they found out she was doing energy work, the whole thing turned into a tempest in a teapot, and the charges were dropped. Even so, we spent a couple of uncomfortable weeks working to clear up the situation.

Ethical issues show up from time to time in any healthcare service and Healing Touch Program is no exception. Dawn Warnaca, acting head of the Healing Touch Professional Association, thought it would be a good idea for all the Healing Touch practitioners and students to be familiar with the laws governing touch in each of their respective states. It occurred to me this is true for all the energy medicine modalities. Thus, the idea for this book was born.

What Constitutes a Professional Practice

Once you accept money, or some form of compensation that has value, for your services you lose your amateur status and enter the world of professional practice and must obey all the laws that govern what you do. As an amateur, you do not have to worry about rules. However, as a professional, all kinds of rules come in to play.

By the way, the IRS considers donations as income and that puts you in the classification of professional. While a tip is also considered income, a gift is not. This is a muddy area and I would suggest talking to a CPA for clarification.

An Important Point

The general rule for most of the country is, whether you are a minister, a nurse, or other healthcare provider, and you receive compensation for energy work via your salary and it is stated as part of your job description, then you can ignore the massage laws. However, if you have a private practice and compensation for your energy work comes directly from the client, you must be in compliance with the massage and counseling laws. Ministers are no longer exempt unless they can prove they have a congregation and compensation comes through their salary from the church. If your "congregation" consists only of clients and you do not conduct traditional types of religious services, then you must be in compliance with the massage laws in your area regarding touch. In Oregon, nurses are now exempt from the massage laws and may have a private energy medicine practice without adhering to the massage laws. At the time of this writing, Oregon is the only state to allow this exemption.

Several nurses spoke to their state legislators and to the Oregon Massage Board, which brought about a change in the laws.

Liability Insurance

Another area of concern is liability insurance for your practice. Most nurses, for example, are covered by insurance for their work as a nurse. However, that insurance may not cover a private practice involving energy work, as it is not a part of the job description. Check with your insurance agent to see if you are covered in your private practice.

Laws Governing Energy Medicine Practitioners

You can get liability insurance through the Healing Touch Professional Association (HTPA). Practitioners from all the energy medicine modalities, such as Reiki and Therapeutic Touch are welcome to join the HTPA. Instructors, students, and practitioners may acquire both general and professional liability insurance through HTPA. This insurance is underwritten by Philadelphia Insurance Companies.

The Reiki Membership Association also offers insurance for its members. It is underwritten by insurance underwriter: Aspen Specialty Insurance Company, wholly owned subsidiary of Aspen Insurance Holdings, LTD.

The International Society for the Study of Subtle Energies and Energy Medicine (ISSEEEM) recently announced they offer professional and general liability insurance for energy medicine practitioners through the Energy Medicine Professional Insurance Associate Member Program. If you cannot find liability insurance within your modality, you can get it through one of these three.

Most common Problem Areas

Energy medicine practitioners and biofield therapists must be in compliance with their state's massage laws. Usually touch is allowed as long as the skin doesn't move. Most states list stroking the skin a massage technique, and require a massage license for the use of stroking techniques. Many states require reflexologists to have a massage license, Florida is very firm on this issue. I have found no laws that regulate practitioners working off the body (no touch).

Problems with counseling have also arisen in some states. Asking a client to tell their story regarding their issue is allowed, to enable the practitioner to choose a course of treatment. However, offering advice about an issue is considered counseling and out of the scope of practice of most energy medicine practitioners, unless the practitioner has a counseling license. Emotional issues are often treated using taping techniques. People using tapping techniques such as Emotional Freedom Technique (EFT), need to be especially careful of staying within their scope of practice.

Licensing versus Certification

Certification is not a license. Certification shows competency in a given discipline or modality. Achieving certification adds credibility to your work and shows you are serious enough about your practice to go the extra mile to offer your clients quality work. However, receiving certification in a given discipline does not mean you have a license to practice that discipline.

Governmental agencies issue licenses. You must show proficiency in your modality, such as massage therapy, usually through passing a test, before you can receive a license. Certification only proves you are proficient in a specific discipline. I don't know of a state that requires testing in any given energy medicine discipline.

Some energy medicine disciplines say they offer licensing. What they are actually doing is granting a license to use their name and often their logo for advertising your practice. It has nothing to do with a governmental license that allows you to legally practice your trade.

Information Subject to Change

Governmental agencies change their contact information and their statutes from time to time. I found two ways to get the information I needed. If you know the name of the state agency (such as the Oregon Board of Massage) you can go to their web site to look for laws governing a massage practice and the exemptions. You can also search for the name of the state legislature, or legislative body of a country, and type in massage or energy healing in the search box of the web page. The web site will then take you to the statutes that regulate the laws in your area. You can do the same for local statutes. Be sure to check for exemptions. A few states actually exempt Healing Touch, Reiki, Therapeutic Touch and Polarity Therapy. Some exempt energy healing without listing examples. I also have noticed that, at times, what the massage board lists for regulations may differ from the actual statutes. I always refer to the state statutes first. However, I did run into a situation where the massage board knew of a change in regulations and the state had yet to put it up on their web site.

By the way, in researching laws concerning energy healers in all states, consent forms always came up. In almost all states they are required if the practitioner wants to protect him or herself, if someone files a complaint.

Laws across the United States and It's Territories

The following entries are copied and pasted directly from each state's statues. I make a few comments here and there for clarification.

Alabama

State of Alabama Board of Massage Therapy
2777 Zelda Road
Montgomery AL 36106
334-420-7233 or 866-873-4664
Fax: 334-263-6115
massagetherapy@alstateboard.com
www.almtbd.state.al.us

Section 34-43-3 of the Alabama Code
13) THERAPEUTIC MASSAGE AND RELATED TOUCH THERAPY MODALITIES. The mobilization of the soft tissue which may include skin, fascia, tendons, ligaments, and muscles, for the purpose of establishing and maintaining good physical condition. The term shall include effleurage, petrissage, tapotement, compression, vibration, stretching, heliotherapy, superficial hot and cold applications, topical applications, or other therapy which involves movement either by hand, forearm, elbow, or foot, for the purpose of therapeutic massage.

Massage therapy may include the external application and use of herbal or chemical preparations and lubricants such as salts, powders, liquids, nonprescription creams, mechanical devises such as T-bars, thumpers, body support systems, heat lamps, hot and cold packs, salt glow, steam cabinet baths or hydrotherapy. The term includes any massage, movement therapy, massage technology, myotherapy, massotherapy, oriental massage techniques, structural integration, or polarity therapy. The term shall not include laser therapy, microwave, injection therapy, manipulation of the joints, or any diagnosis or treatment of an illness that normally involves the practice of medicine, chiropractic, physical therapy, podiatry, nursing, occupational therapy, veterinary, acupuncture, osteopathy, orthopedics, hypnosis, or naturopathics.

Section 34-43-5 of the Alabama Code: Exemptions

(2) Qualified members of other professions who are licensed and regulated under Alabama law while they are in the course of rendering services within the scope of their license or regulation, provided that they do not represent themselves as massage therapists.
(6) Native American healers using traditional healing practices, provided, however, Native American healers who use these practices but apply for a license pursuant to this chapter shall comply with all licensure requirements.

The Alabama Board of Massage Therapy Administrative Code Chapter 532-x-1-02 h defines "massage therapy" as the profession in which the practitioner applies massage techniques and related touch therapies with the intention of positively affecting the health and well-being of the client.

Alabama Board of Examiners in Counseling
950 22nd Street North
Suite 765
Birmingham, AL 35203
205-458-8716 or

800-822-3307
Florence.Hemphill@abec.alabama.gov

Section 34-8A-02
5) PRIVATE PRACTICE OF COUNSELING. Rendering or offering to render to individuals, groups, organizations, or the general public counseling services, in settings of individual or group practice, for a fee, salary, or other compensation, involving the application of principles, methods, or procedures of the counseling profession which include, but are not restricted to:

a. Counseling. To render evaluation and therapy that includes, but is not limited to, providing individual counseling, family counseling, marital counseling, group therapy, school counseling, play therapy, rehabilitation counseling, art therapy, human growth and development counseling, couples counseling, chemical abuse or dependency counseling, career counseling, and vocational disability counseling. The use of specific methods, techniques, or modalities within the practice of a licensed professional counselor is restricted to counselors appropriately trained in the use of these methods, techniques, or modalities. A licensed professional counselor or associate licensed counselor may diagnose and develop treatment plans but shall not attempt to diagnose, prescribe for, treat, or advise client with reference to problems or complaints falling outside the boundaries of counseling services.

b. Appraisal activities. Selecting, administering, scoring, and interpreting instruments designed to assess an individual's aptitudes, attitudes, abilities, achievements, interests, and personal characteristics, but shall not include the use of projective techniques in the assessment of personality.

c. Counseling, guidance, and personnel consulting. Interpreting or reporting upon scientific fact or theory in counseling, guidance, and personnel services to provide assistance in solving some current or potential problems of individuals, groups, or organizations.

d. *Referral activities. The evaluating of data to identify problems and to determine advisability of referral to other specialists.*

e. *Research activities. The designing, conducting, and interpreting of research with human subjects.*

Alaska

Alaska Board of Massage Therapists
PO Box 110806
Juneau AK 99811-0806
Phone: (907) 465-3811
Fax: (907) 465-2974
Email: susan.johnson@alaska.gov
www.legis.state.ak.us

Section 08-61-100
(5) "practice of massage therapy" means the provision, for compensation, of a service involving the systematic manipulation and treatment of the soft tissues, including the muscular and connective tissues of the human body, to enhance the functions of those tissues and promote relaxation and well-being; in this paragraph, "manipulation and treatment"

(A) includes manual techniques applied with the intent to physically affect local soft tissues, such as pressure, friction, stroking, percussion, kneading, vibration, muscular assessment by palpation, range of motion for purposes of demonstrating muscle exertion for muscle flexibility, nonspecific stretching, and application of superficial heat, cold, water, lubricants, or salts;

(B) does not include diagnosis, the prescription of drugs or medicines, the practice of physical therapy, attempts to manipulate any articulation of the body or spine, or mobilization of these articulations by use of a thrusting force.

(4) <u>Exemptions</u>. Numerous practices are exempted from the licensing requirement, including structural integration/Rolfing, energy work, Native American Healing, and massage in the athletic departments of state-funded institutions and schools approved by the Board. Please see section 08.61.080 on pages 6-8 of <u>the law</u> for the full list of exemptions.

Section 08-61-080: Exemptions
(11) person using only light touch, words, and directed movement to deepen awareness of existing patterns of movement in the body as well as to suggest new possibilities of movement or to affect the energy systems:

(12) person performing only the traditional practices of Native American traditional healers;

(13) person practicing only the manipulation of the soft tissues of the hands, feet, or ears and not holding out to be a massage therapist.

Alaska Board of Professional Counselors
P.O. Box 110806
Juneau, AK 99811-0806
(907) 465-2550
Fax: (907) 465-2974
license@alaska.gov
http://commerce.state.ak.us/dnn/cbpl/ProfessionalLicensing/ProfessionalCounselors.aspx

Sec. 08.29.490. Definitions. In this chapter,

(1) "practice of professional counseling" means, subject to (C) of this paragraph, the application of principles, methods, or procedures of the counseling profession to diagnose or treat, other than through the use of projective testing or individually administered intelligence tests, mental and emotional disorders that are referenced in the standard diagnostic nomenclature for individual, group, and organizational therapy, whether cognitive, affective, or behavioral, within the context of human relationships and systems; if otherwise within the scope of this paragraph, "practice of professional counseling" includes

(A) the professional application of evaluation techniques, treatments, and therapeutic services to individuals and groups for the purpose of treating the emotional and mental disorders;

(B) an applied understanding of the dynamics of the individual and of group interactions, along with the application of therapeutic and counseling techniques for the purpose of resolving intrapersonal and interpersonal conflict and changing perceptions, attitudes, and behaviors in the area of human relationships; and

(C) consistent with regulations adopted by the board under AS 08.29.020(a)(4), administration and use of appropriate assessment instruments that measure or diagnose problems or dysfunctions within the course of human growth and development as part of a counseling process or in the development of a treatment plan;

Arizona

Arizona State Board of Massage Therapy
1400 W Washington Street, Suite 300
Phoenix AZ 85007
602-542-8604
info@massageboard.az.gov
www.massageboard.az.gov
http://www.azleg.state.az.us

Arizona State Legislature Formal Document 32-4201 Definitions
5. "Massage therapy" means the following that are undertaken to increase wellness, relaxation, stress reduction, pain relief and postural improvement or provide general or specific therapeutic benefits:
(a) The manual application of compression, stretch, vibration or mobilization of the organs and tissues beneath the dermis, including the components of the musculoskeletal system, peripheral vessels of the circulatory system and fascia, when applied primarily to parts of the body other than the hands, feet and head.
(b) The manual application of compression, stretch, vibration or mobilization using the forearms, elbows, knees or feet or handheld mechanical or electrical devices.
(c) Any combination of range of motion, directed, assisted or passive movements of the joints.

No mention of exemptions.

Arizona Board of Behavioral Health Examiners
3443 North Central Avenue #1700
Phoenix, AZ 85012
602-542-1882
Fax Number: 602-364-0890
http://azbbhe.us/

Counseling: 32-3251. Definitions

8. "Practice of behavioral health" means the practice of marriage and family therapy, professional counseling, social work and substance abuse counseling pursuant to this chapter.

9. "Practice of marriage and family therapy" means the professional application of family systems theories, principles and techniques to treat interpersonal relationship issues and nervous, mental and emotional disorders that are cognitive, affective or behavioral. The practice of marriage and family therapy includes:

(a) Assessment, appraisal and diagnosis.

(b) The use of psychotherapy for the purpose of evaluation, diagnosis and treatment of individuals, couples, families and groups.

10. "Practice of professional counseling" means the professional application of mental health, psychological and human development theories, principles and techniques to:

(a) Facilitate human development and adjustment throughout the human life span.

(b) Assess and facilitate career development.

(c) Treat interpersonal relationship issues and nervous, mental and emotional disorders that are cognitive, affective or behavioral.

(d) Manage symptoms of mental illness.

(e) Assess, appraise, evaluate, diagnose and treat individuals, couples, families and groups through the use of psychotherapy.

32-3271. Exceptions to licensure; jurisdiction

3. A rabbi, priest, minister or member of the clergy of any religious denomination or sect if the activities and services that person performs are within the scope of the performance of the regular or specialized ministerial duties of an established and legally recognizable church, denomination or sect and the person performing the services remains accountable to the established authority of the church, denomination or sect.

4. A member run self-help or self-growth group if no member of the group receives direct or indirect financial compensation.

Arkansas

Arkansas State Board of Massage Therapy
101 East Capitol, Suite 460
P.O. Box 2019
Little Rock AR 72203
Phone: 501-683-1448
Fax: 501-683-1426
info@arkansasmassagetherapy.com
www.arkansasmassagetherapy.com

Arkansas has laws concerning acupuncture, but I couldn't find anything specific concerning field or tapping modalities.
Massage laws:

1. *Terms found in Arkansas Code §17-86-102 are descriptive rather than limiting, and massage therapy includes those techniques which are utilized in all phases of massage and bodywork for the purposes of relaxation, stress reduction, pain relief, injury prevention, injury repair, postural improvement and/or health enhancement. "Massage therapy" means to engage in the practice of any of the following procedures: (A) All massage therapy techniques and procedures, either hands-on or with mechanical devices; (B) Therapeutic application and use of oils, herbal or chemical preparations, lubricants, nonprescription creams, lotions, scrubs, powders, and other spa services; (C) Therapeutic application of hot or cold packs; (D) Hydrotherapy techniques; (E) Heliotherapy; (F) Electrotherapy; (G) Any hands-on bodywork techniques and procedures rising to the level of the techniques and procedures intended to be regulated under this chapter and not covered under specific licensing laws of other boards.*

    I found no mention of exemptions.

Arkansas Board of Examiners in Counseling
101 East Capitol, Suite 104
Little Rock, AR 72201
(501) 683-5800
FAX (501) 683-6349
http://abec.arkansas.gov/

Arkansas Code Annotated 17-27-101
Section 1.9 Definitions
(b) "Counseling/Psychotherapy" means assisting individuals or groups, through the counseling relationship, to develop understanding of personal problems, define goals, and plan action reflecting interests, abilities, aptitudes, and needs. Counseling/ Psychotherapy is the application of mental health, psychological, or human development principles, through cognitive, affective, behavioral or systemic intervention strategies that address wellness, personal growth, or career development, as well as pathology. The terms Counseling/ Psychotherapy are used interchangeably in definitions of mental health activities in counseling textbooks.

California

California Massage Therapy Council
One Capitol Mall, Suite 320
Sacramento, CA 95814
Phone: (916) 669-5336
Fax: (916) 669-5337
www.camtc.org

SB577--California's alternative health care law

SECTION 1.
The Legislature hereby finds and declares all of the following:

a. *Based upon a comprehensive report by the National Institute of Medicine and other studies, including a study published by the New England Journal of Medicine, it is evident that millions of Californians, perhaps more than five million, are presently receiving a substantial volume of health care services from complementary and alternative health care practitioners. Those studies further indicate that individuals utilizing complementary and alternative health care services cut across a wide variety of age, ethnic, socioeconomic, and other demographic categories.*

b. *Notwithstanding the widespread utilization of complementary and alternative medical services by Californians, the provision of many of these services may be in technical violation of the Medical Practice Act (Chapter 5 (commencing with Section 2000) of Division 2 of the Business and Professions Code). Complementary and alternative health care practitioners could therefore be subject to fines, penalties, and the restriction of their practice under the Medical Practice Act even though there is no demonstration that their practices are harmful to the public.*

c. *The Legislature intends, by enactment of this act, to allow access by California residents to complementary and alternative health care practitioners who are not providing services that require medical training* and credentials. The Legislature further finds that these nonmedical complementary and alternative services do not pose a known risk to the health and safety of California residents, and that restricting access to those services due to technical violations of the Medical Practice Act is not warranted.

SECTION 3.
Section 2053.6 is added to the Business and Professions Code, to read:

2053.6.
- a. A person who provides services pursuant to Section 2053.5 that are not unlawful under Section 2051, 2052, or 2053 shall, prior to providing those services, do the following:
    1. Disclose to the client in a written statement using plain language the following information
        - A. That he or she is not a licensed physician
        - B. That the treatment is alternative or complementary to healing arts services licensed by the state.
        - C. That the services to be provided are not licensed by the state.
        - D. The nature of the services to be provided.
        - E. The theory of treatment upon which the services are based.
        - F. His or her educational, training, experience, and other qualifications regarding the services to be provided.
    2. Obtain a written acknowledgement from the client stating that he or she has been provided with the information described in paragraph (1). The client shall be provided with a copy of the written acknowledgement, which shall be maintained by the person providing the service for three years.
- b. The information required by subdivision (a) shall be provided in a language that the client understands.

As of January 1, 2017 all massage therapists must be licensed by the state. AB1147 Section 4601

(e) "Massage" means the scientific manipulation of the soft tissues. For purposes of this chapter, the terms "massage" and "bodywork" shall have the same meaning.

Board of Behavioral Sciences
1625 North Market Blvd, Suite S200
Sacramento, CA 95834
http://www.bbs.ca.gov

§4980.10. ENGAGING IN PRACTICE A person engages in the practice of marriage and family therapy when he or she performs or offers to perform or holds himself or herself out as able to perform this service for remuneration in any form, including donations.

2903. The practice of psychology is defined as rendering or offering to render for a fee to individuals, groups, organizations, or the public any psychological service involving the application of psychological principles, methods, and procedures of understanding, predicting, and influencing behavior, such as the principles pertaining to learning, perception, motivation, emotions, and interpersonal relationships, and the methods and procedures of interviewing, counseling, psychotherapy, behavior modification, and hypnosis, and of constructing, administering, and interpreting tests of mental abilities, aptitudes, interests, attitudes, personality characteristics, emotions and motivations.

Colorado

Office of Legislative Legal Services
200 E Colfax Avenue
Denver CO 80203
(303) 866-2045
http://tornado.state.co.us/

Colorado has enacted laws regarding energy healers. I have listed the most informative ones below. Information about massage laws and counseling laws are not applicable.

Concerning alternative health care practitioners, and, in connection therewith, enacting the "Colorado Natural Health Consumer Protection Act" to provide an exemption from state regulation for unlicensed complementary and alternative health care practitioners, require a person providing complementary and alternative health care services to disclose to clients the person's educational background and the nature of the services to be provided, and prohibit complementary and alternative health care practitioners from engaging in specified activities that only state-regulated health care professionals may perform.

Colorado Revised Statutes Section 1. 6-1-724

>   *(d) Although complementary and alternative health care practitioners are not regulated by the state and are not required to obtain a state-issued license, certification, or registration, the provision of alternative health care services in some circumstances may be interpreted as the provision of a health care service that only a professional who is licensed or otherwise regulated by the state may perform, thereby subjecting complementary and alternative health care practitioners to potential fines, penalties, and restrictions of their practices even though their practices do not pose an imminent and discernable risk of significant harm to public health and safety;*

Laws Governing Energy Medicine Practitioners

(e) Because the state recognizes and values the freedom of consumers to choose their health care providers, including the ability to choose a person who is not regulated by the state, the intent of this section is to protect consumer choice and, in consideration of the public's health and safety, to remove technical barriers to access to unregulated health care practitioners and include appropriate consumer protections and disclosures as required in this section; and

(f) Nothing in this section:

(I) Requires a person engaged in complementary and alternative health care to obtain a license, certification, or registration from the state as long as the person practices within the parameters of this section;

(II) Limits the public's right to access complementary and alternative health care practitioners or the right of an unregulated complementary and alternative health care practitioner to practice.

(3) As used in this section, unless the context otherwise requires:

(a) "Complementary and alternative health care practitioner" means a person who provides complementary and alternative health care services in accordance with this section and who is not licensed, certified, or registered by the state as a health care professional.

(b) (I) "Complementary and alternative health care services" means advice and services:

(A) Within the broad domain of health care and healing arts therapies and methods that are based on complementary and alternative theories of health and wellness, including those that are traditional, cultural, religious, or integrative; and

(B) THAT ARE NOT PROHIBITED BY SUBSECTION (6) OF THIS SECTION.

(II) "COMPLEMENTARY AND ALTERNATIVE HEALTH CARE SERVICES" INCLUDE:

(A) HEALING PRACTICES USING FOOD; FOOD EXTRACTS; DIETARY SUPPLEMENTS, AS DEFINED IN THE FEDERAL "DIETARY SUPPLEMENT HEALTH AND EDUCATION ACT OF 1994", PUB.L. 103-417; NUTRIENTS; HOMEOPATHIC REMEDIES AND PREPARATIONS; AND THE PHYSICAL FORCES OF HEAT, COLD, WATER, TOUCH, SOUND, AND LIGHT;

(B) STRESS REDUCTION HEALING PRACTICES; AND

(C) MIND-BODY AND ENERGETIC HEALING PRACTICES.

(c) "HEALTH CARE PROFESSIONAL" MEANS A PERSON ENGAGED IN A HEALTH CARE PROFESSION FOR WHICH THE STATE REQUIRES THE PERSON TO OBTAIN A LICENSE, CERTIFICATION, OR REGISTRATION UNDER TITLE 12, C.R.S., IN ORDER TO ENGAGE IN THE HEALTH CARE PROFESSION.

(4) THIS SECTION APPLIES TO ANY PERSON WHO IS NOT LICENSED, CERTIFIED, OR REGISTERED BY THE STATE AS A HEALTH CARE PROFESSIONAL AND WHO IS PRACTICING COMPLEMENTARY AND ALTERNATIVE HEALTH CARE SERVICES.

(5) (a) A PERSON WHO IS NOT LICENSED, CERTIFIED, OR REGISTERED BY THE STATE AS A HEALTH CARE PROFESSIONAL AND WHO IS PRACTICING COMPLEMENTARY AND ALTERNATIVE HEALTH CARE SERVICES CONSISTENT WITH THIS SECTION DOES NOT VIOLATE ANY STATUTE RELATING TO A HEALTH CARE PROFESSION OR PROFESSIONAL PRACTICE ACT UNLESS THE PERSON:

(I) ENGAGES IN AN ACTIVITY PROHIBITED IN SUBSECTION (6) OF THIS SECTION; OR

(II) FAILS TO FULFILL THE DISCLOSURE DUTIES SPECIFIED IN SUBSECTION (7) OF THIS SECTION.

Laws Governing Energy Medicine Practitioners

(b) A COMPLEMENTARY AND ALTERNATIVE HEALTH CARE PRACTITIONER WHO ENGAGES IN AN ACTIVITY PROHIBITED BY SUBSECTION (6) OF THIS SECTION IS SUBJECT TO THE ENFORCEMENT PROVISIONS, CIVIL PENALTIES, AND DAMAGES SPECIFIED IN PART 1 OF THIS ARTICLE, IS NO LONGER EXEMPT FROM LAWS REGULATING THE PRACTICE OF HEALTH CARE PROFESSIONALS UNDER TITLE 12, C.R.S., AND MAY BE SUBJECT TO PENALTIES FOR UNAUTHORIZED PRACTICE OF A STATE-REGULATED HEALTH CARE PROFESSION.

(I) INCLUDES PRACTICES WHERE THE PRIMARY PURPOSE IS TO PROVIDE DEEP STROKING MUSCLE TISSUE MASSAGE OF THE HUMAN BODY; AND

(II) EXCLUDES:

(A) STROKING OF THE HANDS, FEET, OR EARS; OR

(B) THE USE OF TOUCH, WORDS, AND DIRECTED MOVEMENT OF A HEALING ART WITHIN THE BODYWORK COMMUNITY, INCLUDING HEALING TOUCH, MIND-BODY CENTERING, ORTHOBIONOMY, REFLEXOLOGY, ROLFING, REIKI, QIGONG, MUSCLE ACTIVATION TECHNIQUES, AND PRACTICES WITH THE PRIMARY PURPOSE OF AFFECTING ENERGY SYSTEMS OF THE HUMAN BODY;

(7) (a) ANY PERSON PROVIDING COMPLEMENTARY AND ALTERNATIVE HEALTH CARE SERVICES IN THIS STATE WHO IS NOT LICENSED, CERTIFIED, OR REGISTERED BY THE STATE AS A HEALTH CARE PROFESSIONAL, IS NOT REGULATED BY A PROFESSIONAL BOARD OR THE DIVISION OF PROFESSIONS AND OCCUPATIONS IN THE DEPARTMENT OF REGULATORY AGENCIES PURSUANT TO TITLE 12, C.R.S., AND IS ADVERTISING OR CHARGING A FEE FOR HEALTH CARE SERVICES SHALL PROVIDE TO EACH CLIENT DURING THE INITIAL CLIENT CONTACT THE FOLLOWING INFORMATION IN A PLAINLY WORDED WRITTEN STATEMENT:

(I) THE COMPLEMENTARY AND ALTERNATIVE HEALTH CARE PRACTITIONER'S NAME, BUSINESS ADDRESS, TELEPHONE NUMBER, AND ANY OTHER CONTACT INFORMATION FOR THE PRACTITIONER;

(II) The fact that the complementary and alternative health care practitioner is not licensed, certified, or registered by the state as a health care professional;

(III) The nature of the complementary and alternative health care services to be provided;

(IV) A listing of any degrees, training, experience, credentials, or other qualifications the person holds regarding the complementary and alternative health care services he or she provides;

(V) A statement that the client should discuss any recommendations made by the complementary and alternative health care practitioner with the client's primary care physician, obstetrician, gynecologist, oncologist, cardiologist, pediatrician, or other board-certified physician; and

(VI) A statement indicating whether or not the complementary and alternative health care practitioner is covered by liability insurance applicable to any injury caused by an act or omission of the complementary and alternative health care practitioner in providing complementary and alternative health care services pursuant to this section.

(b) Before a complementary and alternative health care practitioner provides complementary and alternative health care services for the first time to a client, the complementary and alternative health care practitioner shall obtain a written, signed acknowledgment from the client stating that the client has received the information described in paragraph (a) of this subsection (7). The complementary and alternative health care practitioner shall give a copy of the acknowledgment to the client and shall retain the original or a copy of the acknowledgment for at least two years after the last date of service.

Laws Governing Energy Medicine Practitioners

(c) A COMPLEMENTARY AND ALTERNATIVE HEALTH CARE PRACTITIONER SHALL NOT REPRESENT IN ANY ADVERTISEMENT FOR COMPLEMENTARY AND ALTERNATIVE HEALTH CARE SERVICES THAT THE COMPLEMENTARY AND ALTERNATIVE HEALTH CARE PRACTITIONER IS LICENSED, CERTIFIED, OR REGISTERED BY THE STATE AS A HEALTH CARE PROFESSIONAL.

Connecticut

Connecticut Department of Public Health
Massage Therapist Licensure
410 Capitol Ave., MS # 12 APP
P.O. Box 340308
Hartford, CT 06134
Phone: (860) 509-7603
Fax: (860) 707-1982
Email: dph.alliedhealth@ct.gov
www.ct.gov/dph

Sec. 20-206a. Definitions
(d) "Massage therapy" means the systematic and scientific manipulation and treatment of the soft tissues of the body, by use of pressure, friction, stroking, percussion, kneading, vibration by manual or mechanical means, range of motion and nonspecific stretching. Massage therapy may include the use of oil, ice, hot and cold packs, tub, shower, steam, dry heat, or cabinet baths, for the purpose of, but not limited to, maintaining good health and establishing and maintaining good physical and mental condition. Massage therapy does not encompass (1) diagnosis, the prescribing of drugs or medicines, spinal or other joint manipulations, (2) any service or procedure for which a license to practice medicine, chiropractic, natureopathy, physical therapy, or podiatry is required by law, or (3) Thai yoga practiced by a person who is registered as a yoga teacher with the Yoga Alliance Registry and has completed two hundred hours of training in Thai yoga.

Connecticut Department of Public Health
Professional Counselor Licensing
410 Capitol Ave., MS # 12 APP
P.O. Box 340308
Hartford, CT 06134
Phone: (860) 509-7603

Fax: (860) 707-1982
dph.alliedhealth@ct.gov
www.ct.gov/dph

CONNECTICUT GENERAL STATUTES CHAPTER 383c PROFESSIONAL COUNSELORS Sec. 20-195aa. Definitions: As used in sections 20-195aa to 20-195ee, inclusive: "Professional counseling" means the application, by persons trained in counseling, of established principles of psycho-social development and behavioral science to the evaluation, assessment, analysis, diagnosis and treatment of emotional, behavioral or interpersonal dysfunction or difficulties that interfere with mental health and human development. "Professional counseling" includes, but is not limited to, individual, group, marriage and family counseling, functional assessments for persons adjusting to a disability, appraisal, crisis intervention and consultation with individuals or groups.
(c) No license as a professional counselor shall be required of the following: (1) A person who furnishes uncompensated assistance in an emergency; (2) a clergyman, priest, minister, rabbi or practitioner of any religious denomination accredited by the religious body to which the person belongs and settled in the work of the ministry, provided the activities that would otherwise require a license as a professional counselor are within the scope of ministerial duties; (3) a sexual assault counselor, as defined in section 52-146k; (4) a person participating in uncompensated group or individual counseling; (5) a person with a master's degree in a health-related or human services-related field employed by a hospital, as defined in subsection (b) of section 19a-490, performing services in accordance with section 20-195aa under the supervision of a person licensed by the state in one of the professions identified in subparagraphs (A) to (F), inclusive, of subdivision (2) of subsection (a) of section 20-195dd; (6) a person licensed or certified by any agency of this state and performing services within the scope of practice for which licensed or certified; (7) a student, intern or trainee pursing a course of study in counseling in a regionally accredited institution of higher education, provided the activities that would otherwise require a license as a professional counselor are performed under supervision and constitute a part of supervised course of study; (8) a person employed by an

institution of higher education to provide academic counseling in conjunction with the institution's programs and services; or (9) a vocational rehabilitation counselor, job counselor, credit counselor, consumer counselor or any other counselor or psychoanalyst who does not purport to be a counselor whose primary service is the application of established principles of psycho-social development and behavioral science to the evaluation, assessment, analysis and treatment of emotional, behavioral or interpersonal dysfunction or difficulties that interfere with mental health and human development.

Delaware

Delaware Board of Massage and Bodywork
Cannon Building, Suite 203
861 Silver Lake Blvd.
Dover DE 19904
(302) 744-4500
Customerservice.dpr@state.de.us
www.dpr.delaware.gov/boards/massagebodyworks/

TITLE 24: Professions and Occupations

CHAPTER 53. MASSAGE AND BODYWORK

Subchapter I. Board of Massage and Bodywork

70 Del.Laws.c.582
5302: Definitions
(6) "Practice of massage and bodywork" shall mean a system of structured touch applied to the superficial or deep tissue, muscle, or connective tissue, by applying pressure with manual means. Such application may include, but is not limited to, friction, gliding, rocking, tapping, kneading, or nonspecific stretching, whether or not aided by massage oils or the application of hot and cold treatments. The practice of massage and bodywork is designed to promote general relaxation, enhance circulation, improve joint mobilization and/or relieve stress and muscle tension, and to promote a general sense of well-being.
The Delaware Board of Massage and Bodywork Statutory Authority: 24 Del.C.Section 5305(1) 24 DE Admin. Code 5305(1)

2.4 "Massage and bodywork" includes, but is not limited to, the following practices or modalities:Acupressure, Chair Massage, Clinical aroma therapy, Craniosacal therapy, Deep Tissue Massage Therapy, Hellerwork, Manual Lymphatic Drainage, Massage Therapy, Myofascial Release Therapy, Neuromuscular

Therapy, Process Acupressure, Reflexology, Rolfing, Shiatsu, Swedish Massage Therapy, Trager, Visceral Manipulation.

The Board of Professional Counselors of Mental Health and Chemical Dependency Professionals does not define a counselor.

District of Columbia

District of Columbia Board of Massage Therapy
Department of Health
825 North Capitol Street NE
Washington, DC 20002
(202) 442-5955
doh@dc.gov
www.doh.dc.gov

Title 17 District of Columbia Municipal Regulations for Massage Therapy 7599.1: Definitions Incidental use - means soft tissue manipulation performed as part of movement reeducation, energy healing, or other modality in which the soft tissue manipulation is not the central aim of the treatment, but is performed occasionally to facilitate the nonmassage therapy practice.

Massage techniques - means any touching or pressure with the intent of providing healing or therapeutic benefits through soft tissue manipulation. Massage techniques include, but are not limited to, Rolfing, Neuromuscular Therapy, Shiatsu or acupressure, Trigger Point massage, Trager, Tui na, Reflexology, Thai Massage, deep tissue massage, Myofascial Release, Lymphatic Drainage, Craniosacral, Polarity, Reiki, Swedish Massage, and Therapeutic Touch. Massage techniques may be performed in any postural position including seated massage and techniques performed on clothed clients.

Therapeutic - means having a positive affect on the health and well-being of the client.

Professional Counseling
Department of Health
899 North Capitol Street, NE, Washington, DC 20002
Phone: (202) 442-5955
Fax: (202) 442-4795
Email:doh@dc.gov

6699 DEFINITIONS 6699.1 When used in these regulations, the following terms shall have the following meanings ascribed: Act – the District of Columbia Health Occupations Revision Act of 1985, D.C. Law 6-99, as amended.

Practice of professional counseling – engaging in counseling activities, for compensation, by a person who represents, by title or description of services, that he or she is a "professional counselor" or "licensed professional counselor," and includes the processes of: (a) conducting assessments for the purpose of determining treatment goals and objectives; (b) assisting clients through a professional relationship to achieve effective mental, emotional, physical, social, educational, or career development and adjustment throughout the life span; and (c) using counseling treatment interventions to facilitate human development and to identify and remediate mental, emotional, or behavioral conditions and associated difficulties which interfere with functional wellness.

Florida

Florida Department of Health Board of Massage Therapy
4052 Bald Cypress Way Bin C-06
Tallahassee FL32399-3257
(850) 245-4146
info@floridsmassagethreapy.gov
www.floridasmassagetherapy.gov

480,033 Definitions
(3) "Massage" means the manipulation of the soft tissues of the human body with the hand, foot, arm, or elbow, whether or not such manipulation is aided by hydrotherapy, including colonic irrigation, or thermal therapy; any electrical or mechanical device; or the application to the human body of a chemical or herbal preparation.
I couldn't find it in the statutes, but according to the **Florida Department of Health Board of Massage Therapy,** *practitioners of reflexology and reiki must have a massage license. I found nothing concerning other energy healing modalities.*

Florida Board of Psychology
4052 Bald Cypress Way Bin C-05
Tallahassee FL32399-3255
(850) 245-4373
info@floridspsychology.gov
www. floridspsychology.gov

490.003 Definitions
   (4) "Practice of psychology" means the observations, description, evaluation, interpretation, and modification of human behavior, by the use of scientific and applied psychological principles, methods, and procedures, for the purpose of describing, preventing, alleviating, or eliminating symptomatic, maladaptive, or undesired behavior and of enhancing interpersonal behavioral health and mental or psychological health. The ethical practice of psychology includes, but is not limited to, psychological testing and the evaluation or assessment of personal characteristics

such as intelligence, personality, abilities, interests, aptitudes, and neuropsychological functioning, including evaluation of mental competency to manage one's affairs and to participate in legal proceedings; counseling, psychoanalysis, all forms of psychotherapy, sex therapy, hypnosis, biofeedback, and behavioral analysis and therapy; psychoeducational evaluation, therapy, remediation, and consultation; and use of psychological methods to diagnose and treat mental, nervous, psychological, marital, or emotional disorders, illness, or disability, alcoholism and substance abuse, and disorders of habit or conduct, as well as the psychological aspects of physical illness, accident, injury, or disability, including neuropsychological evaluation, diagnosis, prognosis, etiology, and treatment.

(a) Psychological services may be rendered to individuals, couples, families, groups, and the public without regard to place of service.

(b) The use of specific modalities within the practice of psychology is restricted to psychologists appropriately trained in the use of such modalities.

(c) The practice of psychology shall be construed within the meaning of this definition without regard to whether payment is requested or received for services rendered. 490.014 Exemptions

(f) Is a rabbi, priest, minister, or member of the clergy of any religious denomination or sect when engaging in activities which are within the scope of the performance of his or her regular or specialized ministerial duties and for which no separate charge is made, or when such activities are performed, with or without charge, for or under the auspices or sponsorship, individually or in conjunction with others, of an established and legally cognizable church, denomination, or sect, and when the person rendering service remains accountable to the established authority thereof.

Nursing 464.022 Exceptions.—No provision of this part shall be construed to prohibit:
(9) The rendering of nursing services on a fee-for-service basis, or the reimbursement for nursing services directly to a nurse rendering such services by any government program, commercial insurance company, hospital or medical services plan, or any other third-party payor.

Georgia

Georgia Board of Massage Therapy
237 Coliseum Drive
Macon GA 31217
478-207-2440
www.sos.ga.gov/plb/massage/

43-24A-3. Definitions
(8) "Massage therapy" means the application of a system of structured touch, pressure, movement, and holding to the soft tissue of the body in which the primary intent is to enhance or restore health and well-being. The term includes complementary methods, including without limitation the external application of water, superficial heat, superficial cold, lubricants, salt scrubs, or other topical preparations and the use of commercially available electromechanical devices which do not require the use of transcutaneous electrodes and which mimic or enhance the actions possible by the hands; the term also includes determining whether massage therapy is appropriate or contraindicated, or whether referral to another health care provider is appropriate. Massage therapy shall not include the use of ultrasound, fluidotherapy, laser, and other methods of deep thermal modalities 43-24A-19. Exceptions
(5) A person who restricts his or her practice to the manipulation of the soft tissue of the human body to hands, feet, or ears who does not have the client disrobe and does not hold himself or herself out as a massage therapist; (6) A person who uses touch, words, and directed movement to deepen awareness of existing patterns of movement in the body as well as to suggest new possibilities of movement while engaged within the scope of practice of a profession with established standards and ethics, provided that his or her services are not designated or implied to be massage or massage therapy;
(8) A person who uses touch to affect the energy systems, polarity, acupoints, or Qi meridians, also known as channels of energy, of the human body while engaged within the scope of practice of a profession with established standards and ethics, provided that his or her services are not designated or implied to be massage or massage therapy;

Psychology

43-39-7 Exemptions

(6) Nothing in this chapter shall be construed to prohibit any person from engaging in the lawful practice of medicine, nursing, professional counseling, social work, and marriage and family therapy, as provided for under other state law, provided that such person shall not use the title "psychologist" nor imply that he or she is a psychologist;

Guam

Guam Board of Allied Health Examiners
651 Legacy Square Commercial Complex S.
Rte. 10, Suite 9, Mangilao, Guam 96913
671/735-7406/8
671/735-7413
217) 785-0800
(217) 782-7645 fax
www.idfpr.com/dpr/who/prfcns.asp

122303. Definitions
(3) 'Massage Therapy' means utilizing at least one (1) or variations of the following procedures applied by manual means: touching, tapping, stroking, friction, kneading, vibration, compression, percussion, and energy balancing, to enhance the maintenance of good health and as a complement to other health supportive processes;
122304. Exclusions from Practice of Massage.
(3) The providing of any service or procedure for which a license to practice medicine or chiropractic or physical therapy or nursing is otherwise required by law;

10 GCA HEALTH AND SAFETY CH. 12 MEDICAL PRACTICES
(h) Therapy means planned intervention to help the client enlarge competencies and increase problem solving skills and coping abilities. Therapy can be used interchangeably with counseling and psychotherapy. Psychotherapy means a specialized, formal interaction between an Individual, Marriage and Family Therapist or other Mental Health Professionals, and a client (an individual, couple, family or group) in which a therapeutic relationship is established to help resolve symptoms of mental disorder, psychosocial stress, relationship problems, and enhance problem solving skills and coping abilities.

(b) Nothing in these rules and regulations shall be construed to prevent qualified members of other professional groups, such as clinical psychology, school psychology,

counseling psychology, social work or ordained clergy from doing work of a counseling nature consistent with their training and consistent with any code of ethics of their respective professions; provided, however, that they do not hold themselves out to the public by any of the following titles: (1) individual therapist; (2) counselor; (3) marriage therapist; (4) family therapist; (5) psychotherapist; or (6) any combination thereof.

Hawaii

Department of Commerce and Consumer Affairs
Professional & Vocational Licensing
Hawaii State Board of Massage Therapy
Hawaii State Board of Psychology
King Kalakaua Building
335 Merchant Street, room 301
Honolulu, Hawaii 96813
(808) 586-3000
pvl@dcca.hawaii.gov
http://cca.hawaii.gov/pvl/boards/massage/statute_rules/

452-1 Definitions
"Massage", "massage therapy", and "Hawaiian massage" commonly known as lomilomi, means any method of treatment of the superficial soft parts of the body, consisting of rubbing, stroking, tapotement, pressing, shaking, or kneading with the hands, feet, elbow, or arms, and whether or not aided by any mechanical or electrical apparatus, appliances, or supplementary aids such as rubbing alcohol, liniments, antiseptics, oils, powder, creams, lotions, ointments, or other similar preparations commonly used in this practice. Any mechanical or electrical apparatus used as described in this chapter shall be approved by the United States Food and Drug Administration.

452-21 To whom provisions in this chapter shall not apply. Nothing in this chapter shall prohibit service in case of emergency, or domestic administration, without compensation, nor services by persons holding any valid license, permit, or certificate dealing with the healing arts, nor services by barbers, hairdressers, cosmeticians, and cosmetologists lawfully carrying on their particular profession or business under any existing law of this State.

465-1 Definitions
"Practice of psychology" means the observation, description, evaluation, interpretation, or modification of human behavior by the application of psychological

principles, methods, or procedures, for the purpose of preventing or eliminating symptomatic, maladaptive, or undesired behavior and of enhancing interpersonal relationships, work and life adjustment, personal effectiveness, behavioral health, and mental health. The practice of psychology includes, but is not limited to, psychological testing and the evaluation or assessment of personal characteristics, such as intelligence, personality, abilities, interests, aptitudes, and neuropsychological functioning; counseling, psychoanalysis, psychotherapy, hypnosis, biofeedback, and behavior analysis and therapy; diagnosis and treatment of mental and emotional disorder or disability, alcoholism and substance abuse, and disorders of habit or conduct, as well as of the psychological aspects of physical illness, accident, injury, or disability; and psychoeducational evaluation, therapy, remediation, and consultation. Psychological services may be rendered to individuals, families, groups, organizations, institutions, and the public. The practice of psychology shall be construed within the meaning of this definition without regard to whether payment is received for services rendered.

465-3 Exemptions

(5) Any person who is a member of another profession licensed under the laws of this jurisdiction to render or advertise services, including psychotherapy, within the scope of practice as defined in the statutes or rules regulating the person's professional practice; provided that, notwithstanding section 465-1, the person does not represent the person's self to be a psychologist or does not represent that the person is licensed to practice psychology; (6) Any person who is a member of a mental health profession not requiring licensure; provided that the person functions only within the person's professional capacities; and provided further that the person does not represent the person to be a psychologist, or the person's services as psychological; (7) Any person who is a duly recognized member of the clergy; provided that the person functions only within the person's capacities as a member of the clergy; and provided further that the person does not represent the person to be a psychologist, or the person's services as psychological;

Laws Governing Energy Medicine Practitioners

Nursing
457-13 Exemptions
(5) The practice of nursing in connection with healing by prayer or spiritual means alone in accordance with the tenets and practice of any well recognized church or religious denomination, provided that no person practicing such nursing claims to practice as a registered nurse or a licensed practical nurse

Idaho

Idaho State Board of Massage Therapy
700 W. State Street
Boise, ID 83702.
(208) 334-3233
mas@ibol.idaho.gov

54-4002. Definitions
   "*Practice of massage therapy*" *means the application of a system of structured touch, pressure, movement and holding of the soft tissues of the human body. The application may include:*
(a) Pressure, friction, stroking, rocking, kneading, percussion, or passive or active stretching within the normal anatomical range of movement;
54-4003. Exemptions
(e) Persons who restrict their practice to manipulation of the soft tissues of the human body to the hands, feet or ears and do not hold themselves out to be massage therapists or to do massage or massage therapy.
(f) Nothing in this chapter shall be construed to prevent or restrict the practice of any person in this state who uses touch to affect the energy systems, acupoints or qi meridians, channels of energy, of the human body while engaged within the scope of practice of a profession, provided that their services are not designated or implied to be massage or massage therapy. Such practices include, but are not limited to, polarity, polarity therapy, polarity bodywork therapy, Asian bodywork therapy, acupressure, jin shin do®, qi gong, reiki and shiatsu.

Idaho Bureau of Occupational Licenses
Idaho Licensing Board of Professional Counselors and Marriage and Family Therapists
700 W State Street
Boise ID 83702
Fax - (208) 334-3945
Phone - (208) 334-3233
E-mail - ibol@ibol.idaho.gov
www.ibol.idaho.gov

Counseling
54-3401. DEFINITIONS.

(10) "Practice of professional counseling" means the application of mental health, psychological, and human development principles in order to facilitate human development and adjustment throughout the life span; prevent, assess, and treat mental, emotional or behavioral disorders and associated distresses which interfere with mental health; conduct assessments for the purpose of establishing treatment goals and objectives; and plan, implement and evaluate treatment plans using counseling treatment interventions. The practice of professional counseling also means the application of cognitive, affective, behavioral, and systemic counseling strategies across the continuum of care. It includes principles of development, wellness and pathology that reflect a contemporary society. Such interventions are specifically implemented in the context of a professional counseling setting.

The practice of professional counseling includes, but is not limited to:
(a) Individual, group, couples, family counseling and therapy;
(b) Assessment;
(c) Crisis intervention;
(d) Treatment of persons with mental and emotional disorders including, but not limited to, addictive disorders;
(e) Guidance and consulting to facilitate normal growth and development, including educational and career development;
(f) Utilization of functional assessment and counseling for persons requesting assistance in adjustment to a disability;
(g) Consulting;
(h) Research; and
(i) Referral.

The use of specific methods, techniques, or modalities within the practice of professional counseling is restricted to professional counselors appropriately trained in the use of such methods, techniques or modalities.

Illinois

Illinois Department of Financial and Professional Regulations
Massage Therapy Licensure
320 W. Washington Street, 3rd Floor
Springfield IL 62786
(800) 560-6420
(217) 785-0800
(217) 782-7645 fax
www.idfpr.com/dpr/who/prfcns.asp

225 ILCS 57/10 Definitions
"Massage" or "massage therapy" means a system of structured palpation or movement of the soft tissue of the body. The system may include, but is not limited to, techniques such as effleurage or stroking and gliding, petrissage or kneading, tapotement or percussion, friction, vibration, compression, and stretching activities as they pertain to massage therapy. These techniques may be applied by a licensed massage therapist with or without the aid of lubricants, salt or herbal preparations, hydromassage, thermal massage, or a massage device that mimics or enhances the actions possible by human hands. The purpose of the practice of massage, as licensed under this Act, is to enhance the general health and well-being of the mind and body of the recipient. "Massage" does not include the diagnosis of a specific pathology. "Massage" does not include those acts of physical therapy or therapeutic or corrective measures that are outside the scope of massage therapy practice as defined in this Section.

Section 25: Exemptions
    (e) Nothing in this Act prohibits practitioners that do not involve intentional soft tissue manipulation, including but not limited to Alexander Technique, Feldenkrais, Reike, and Therapeutic Touch, from practicing.
    (f) Practitioners of certain service marked bodywork approaches that do involve intentional soft tissue manipulation, including but not limited to Rolfing, Trager Approach, Polarity Therapy, and Orthobionomy, are exempt from this Act

if they are approved by their governing body based on a minimum level of training, demonstration of competency, and adherence to ethical standards.

(g) Practitioners of Asian bodywork approaches are exempt from this Act if they are members of the American Organization of Bodywork Therapies of Asia as certified practitioners or if they are approved by an Asian bodywork organization based on a minimum level of training, demonstration of competency, and adherence to ethical standards set by their governing body.

(h) Practitioners of other forms of bodywork who restrict manipulation of soft tissue to the feet, hands, and ears, and who do not have the client disrobe, such as reflexology, are exempt from this Act.

Professional Counselor Licensing and Disciplinary Board
320 W. Washington Street, 3rd Floor
Springfield IL 62786
(217) 785-0800
(217) 782-7645 fax
www.idfpr.com/dpr/who/prfcns.asp

225 ILCS 107/10, 135/15 CHAPTER 225 PROFESSIONS AND OCCUPATIONS

"Professional counseling" means the provision of services to individuals, couples, groups, families, and organizations in any one or more of the fields of professional counseling. "Professional counseling" includes the therapeutic process of: (i) conducting assessments and diagnosing for the purpose of establishing treatment goals and objectives and (ii) planning, implementing, and evaluating treatment plans using treatment interventions to facilitate human development and to identify and remediate mental, emotional, or behavioral disorders and associated distresses that interfere with mental health.

Professional counseling may also include clinical professional counseling as long as it is not conducted in independent private practice as defined in this Act.

"Clinical professional counseling" means the provision of professional counseling and mental health services, which includes, but is not limited to, the application

of clinical counseling theory and techniques to prevent and alleviate mental and emotional disorders and psychopathology and to promote optimal mental health, rehabilitation, treatment, testing, assessment, and evaluation. "Clinical professional counseling" may include the practice of professional counseling as defined in this Act. It also includes clinical counseling and psychotherapy in a professional relationship to assist individuals, couples, families, groups, and organizations to alleviate emotional disorders, to understand conscious and unconscious motivation, to resolve emotional, relationship, and attitudinal conflicts, and to modify behaviors that interfere with effective emotional, social, adaptive, and intellectual functioning.

"Volunteer" means a person performing services without compensation for a nonprofit organization, a nonprofit corporation, a hospital, a governmental entity, or a private business, other than reimbursement for actual expenses incurred. "Volunteer" includes a person serving as a director, officer, trustee, or direct service volunteer.

(225 ILCS 135/15)

(a) This Act does not prohibit any persons legally regulated in this State by any other Act from engaging in the practice for which they are authorized as long as they do not represent themselves by the title of "genetic counselor" or "licensed genetic counselor". This Act does not prohibit the practice of nonregulated professions whose practitioners are engaged in the delivery of human services as long as these practitioners do not represent themselves as or use the title of "genetic counselor" or "licensed genetic counselor".

(f) Duly recognized members of any religious organization shall not be restricted from functioning in their ministerial capacity provided they do not represent themselves as being genetic counselors or as providing genetic counseling.

Indiana

Indiana Professional Licensing Agency
Indiana State Board of Massage Therapy
402 W Washington Street Room W072
Indianapolis, Indiana 46204
:317-234-8800
pla14@pla.in.gov

IC 25-21.8-1-4"Massage therapy" Sec. 4. "Massage therapy":(1) means the application of massage techniques on the human body;(2) includes:(A) the use of touch, pressure, percussion, kneading, movement, positioning, nonspecific stretching, stretching within the normal anatomical range of movement, and holding, with or without the use of massage devices that mimic or enhance manual measures; and(B) the external application of heat, cold, water, ice, stones, lubricants, abrasives, and topical preparations that are not classified as prescription drugs.

Behavioral and Human Services Licensing Board
402 W Washington Street Room W072
Indianapolis, Indiana 46204
(317) 234-2054
pla8@pla.IN.gov

IC 25-23.6-1-3.6"Counseling"Sec. 3.6. "Counseling" means techniques used to help individuals learn how to solve problems and make decisions related to personal growth, vocational, family, social, and other interpersonal concerns. As added by P.L.147-1997, SEC.17
IC 25-23.6-1-7.5"Practice of mental health counseling" Sec. 7.5. "Practice of mental health counseling" means a specialty that:(1) uses counseling and psychotherapeutic techniques based on principles, methods, and procedures of counseling that assist people in identifying and resolving personal, social, vocational, intrapersonal, and interpersonal concerns;(2) uses counseling to evaluate and treat emotional and mental problems and conditions in a variety of settings, including mental

and physical health facilities, child and family service agencies, or private practice, and including the use of accepted evaluation classifications, including classifications from the American Psychiatric Association's Diagnostic and Statistica lManual of Mental Disorders (DSM-IV) as amended and supplemented, but only to the extent of the counselor's education, training, experience, and scope of practice as established by this article;(3) administers and interprets appraisal instruments that the mental health counselor is qualified to employ by virtue of the counselor's education, training, and experience;(4) uses information and community resources for personal, social, or vocational development;(5) uses individual and group techniques for facilitating problem solving, decision making, and behavioral change;(6) uses functional assessment and vocational planning guidance for persons requesting assistance in adjustment to a disability or disabling condition;(7) uses referrals for individuals who request counseling services; and(8) uses and interprets counseling research. The term does not include diagnosis (as defined in IC 25-22.5-1-1.1(c))

Iowa

Iowa Department of Public Health
Bureau of Professional Licensure
Iowa Board of Massage Therapy
Lucas State Office Bldg., 5th Floor
321 East 12th Street
Des Moines, IA 50319-0075
Phone (515) 281-0254
FAX (515) 281-3121

152C.1 Definitions
healing art of massage therapy under this chapter. 3. "Massage therapy" means performance for compensation of massage, myotherapy, massotherapy, bodywork, bodywork therapy, or therapeutic massage including hydrotherapy, superficial hot and cold applications, vibration and topical applications, or other therapy which involves manipulation of the muscle and connective tissue of the body, excluding osseous tissue, to treat the muscle tonus system for the purpose of enhancing health, muscle relaxation, increasing range of motion, reducing stress, relieving pain, or improving circulation. 4. "Reflexology" means manipulation of the soft tissues of the human body which is restricted to the hands, feet, or ears, performed by persons who do not hold themselves out to be massage therapists or to be performing massage therapy 152C.9 Exemptions.
5. Persons practicing reflexology. 6. Persons engaged within the scope of practice of a profession with established standards and ethics utilizing touch, words, and directed movement to deepen awareness of existing patterns of movement in the body as well as to suggest new possibilities of movement, provided that the practices performed or services rendered are not designated or implied to be massage therapy. Such practices include, but are not limited to, the Feldenkrais method, the Trager approach, and mind-body centering. 7. Persons engaged within the scope of practice of a profession with established standards and ethics in which touch is limited to that which is essential for palpitation and affectation of the human

energy system, provided that the practices performed or services rendered are not designated or implied to be massage therapy.

Iowa Department of Public Health
Iowa Board of Behavioral Science
Lucas State Office Bldg., 5th Floor
321 East 12th Street
Des Moines, IA 50319-0075
Phone (515) 281-0254
FAX (515) 281-3121

154D.1 Definitions.
6. "Mental health counseling" means the provision of counseling services involving assessment, referral, consultation, and the application of counseling, human development principles, learning theory, group dynamics, and the etiology of maladjustment and dysfunctional behavior to individuals, families, and groups.
154D.4 Exemptions. 1. This chapter and chapter 147 do not prevent qualified members of other professions, including but not limited to nurses, psychologists, social workers, physicians, physician assistants, attorneys at law, or members of the clergy, from providing or advertising that they provide services of a marital and family therapy or mental health counseling nature consistent with the accepted standards of their respective professions, but these persons shall not use a title or description denoting that they are licensed marital and family therapists or licensed mental health counselors.

Kansas

Kansas Board of Nursing
Landon State Office Building, Suite 1051
900 SW Jackson Street
Topeka KS 66612-1230
785-296-4929
Fax: 785-296-3929
www.ksbn.org

At the time of this writing Kansas does not have clear cut laws concerning massage or energy healing. Plans for a massage board are under discussion. I found the following under nursing regulations.

2014 Kansas Statutes
65-2901. Definitions. As used in article 29 of chapter 65 of the Kansas Statutes Annotated, and amendments thereto: (a) "Physical therapy" means examining, evaluating and testing individuals with mechanical, anatomical, physiological and developmental impairments, functional limitations and disabilities or other health and movementrelated conditions in order to determine a diagnosis solely for physical therapy, prognosis, plan of therapeutic intervention and to assess the ongoing effects of physical therapy intervention. Physical therapy also includes alleviating impairments, functional limitations and disabilities by designing, implementing and modifying therapeutic interventions that may include, but are not limited to, therapeutic exercise; functional training in community or work integration or reintegration; manual therapy; therapeutic massage; prescription, application and, as appropriate, fabrication of assistive, adaptive, orthotic, prosthetic, protective and supportive devices and equipment; airway clearance techniques; integumentary protection and repair techniques; debridement and wound care; physical agents or modalities; mechanical and electrotherapeutic modalities; patient-related instruction; reducing the risk of injury, impairments, functional limitations and disability, including the promotion and maintenance of fitness,

health and quality of life in all age populations and engaging in administration, consultation, education and research. Physical therapy also includes the care and services provided by a physical therapist or a physical therapist assistant under the direction and supervision of a physical therapist who is licensed pursuant to article 29 of chapter 65 of the Kansas Statutes Annotated, and amendments thereto. Physical therapy does not include the use of roentgen rays and radium for diagnostic and therapeutic purposes, the use of electricity for surgical purposes, including cauterization, the practice of any branch of the healing arts and the making of a medical diagnosis.

65-2872. Persons not engaged in the practice of the healing arts. *The practice of the healing arts shall not be construed to include the following persons:*
(c) The members of any church practicing their religious tenets provided they shall not be exempt from complying with all public health regulations of the state.
(e) Students upon the completion of at least three years study in an accredited healing arts school and who, as a part of their academic requirements for a degree, serve a preceptorship not to exceed 180 days under the supervision of a licensed practitioner.
(h) Persons in the general fields of psychology, education and social work, dealing with the social, psychological and moral well-being of individuals and/or groups provided they do not use drugs and do not hold themselves out to be the physicians, surgeons, osteopathic physicians or chiropractors.
(m) Nurses practicing their profession when licensed and practicing under and in accordance with the provisions of article 11 of chapter 65 of the Kansas Statutes Annotated, and amendments thereto, and any interpretation thereof by the supreme court of this state.
(o) Every act or practice falling in the field of the healing art, not specifically excepted herein, shall constitute the practice thereof.

65-4202. Definitions.
(2) require an application of techniques and procedures that involve understanding of cause and effect and the safeguarding of life and health of the patient and others; and

Laws Governing Energy Medicine Practitioners

(3) require the performance of duties that are necessary to facilitate rehabilitation of the patient or are necessary in the physical, therapeutic and psychiatric care of the patient and require close work with persons licensed to practice medicine and surgery, psychiatrists, psychologists, rehabilitation therapists, social workers, registered nurses, and other professional personnel.

Kentucky

Kentucky Board of Licensure for Massage Therapy
911 Leawood Drive
Frankfort KY 40601
502-782-8808 (Telephone)
502-696-5230 (Fax)
JessicaA.Parker@ky.gov
http://lrc.ky.gov.

309.350 Definitions for KRS 309.350 to 309.364. As used in KRS 309.350 to 309.364 unless the context otherwise requires: (3) "
(4) "Feldenkrais Method" means a system of somatic education in which touch and words are used to eliminate faulty habits, learn new patterns of self-organization and action, and improve a persons own functional movement patterns. The method is based on principles of physics, biomechanics and an understanding of, or learning about, human development. The practice is federally trademarked and requires permission from the Feldenkrais Guild to use the term and methodology;
(6) "Polarity therapy" means diverse applications affecting the human energy system. These applications include energetic approaches to somatic contact, verbal facilitation, nutrition, exercise, and health education. Polarity therapy does not make medical claims, diagnose physical ailments, or allow prescription of medications. Standards for schools, education, and practice, the administration of a code of ethics, and a registration process are provided by the American Polarity Therapy Association;
(7) "Practice of massage therapy" means the application, by a massage therapist licensed by the board, of a system of structured touch, pressure, movement, and holding to the soft tissues of the human body with the intent to enhance or restore the health and well-being of the client. The practice includes the external application of water, heat, cold, lubricants, salt scrubs, or other topical preparations; use of electromechanical devices that mimic or enhance the actions of the hands; and determination of whether massage therapy is appropriate or contraindicated, or whether referral to another health care practitioner is appropriate; and
(8) "Trager Approach" means a form of movement education that uses subtle directed movements and the skilled touch of a practitioner. The Trager Approach

Laws Governing Energy Medicine Practitioners

combines physical movement with sensory awareness and internal imagery designed to increase the client's self-awareness and generate physiological changes in the body tissues so as to allow the client to experience a new way of moving his or her body. The practice is federally trademarked.

309.352 Scope of KRS 309.350 to 309.364. KRS 309.350 to 309.364 shall not preclude:

(4) Persons who restrict manipulation of the soft tissues of the human body to the hands, feet, or ears, and do not hold themselves out to be massage therapists;

(5) Persons who use procedures within the scope of practice of their profession, which has established standards and ethics, provided that their services use touch, words, and directed movement to deepen awareness of existing patterns of movement in the body as well as to suggest new possibilities of movement while engaged, but who are not designated or implied to administer massage or to be massage therapists. These practices include, but are not limited to, the Feldenkrais Method and the Trager Approach;

(6) Persons engaged within the scope of practice of a profession with established standards and ethics in which touch is limited to what is essential for palpation and affecting of the human energy system, provided that their services are not designated or implied to be massage or massage therapy. These practices include but are not limited to polarity therapy;

(9) Practitioners of the following occupations and professions regulated by state law while engaging in the practices for which they are duly licensed and while not holding themselves out to be massage therapists:

(c) Registered nurses and practical nurses regulated under KRS Chapter 314;

Office of Occupations and Professions
Kentucky Board of Licensed Professional Counselors
911 Leawood Drive
Frankfort, KY 40601
502-564-3296, ext. 227
Fax: 502-564-4818
diana.jarboe@ky.gov
www.lpc.ky.gov

335.500 Definitions
(5) "Practice of professional counseling" means professional counseling services that involve the application of mental health counseling and developmental principles, methods, and procedures, including assessment, evaluation, treatment planning, amelioration, and remediation of adjustment problems and emotional disorders, to assist individuals or groups to achieve more effective personal, social, educational, or career development and adjustment;

335.505 Prohibition against unlicensed practice of professional counseling -- No limitation on activities of specified service providers. (1) No person shall engage in the practice of professional counseling or present in a way as to imply or would reasonably be deemed to imply licensure to practice professional counseling unless the person has first been issued a valid license by the board.

(3) Subsection (1) of this section shall not be construed to alter, amend, or interfere with the practice of those who engage in employment counseling, job placement counseling, vocational rehabilitation counseling, victim counseling or advocacy, pastoral counseling based on any tenet of one's religious beliefs, or school counseling.

Louisiana

Louisiana Board of Massage Therapy
2645 O'Neal Lane Bldg. C, Ste. E
Baton Rouge, LA
70816
(225) 756-3488
Fax: (225) 756-3493
admin@labmt.org

3552. Definitions
(10) "Practice of massage therapy" means the manipulation of soft tissue for the purpose of maintaining good health and establishing and maintaining good physical condition. The practice of massage therapy shall include advertising or offering to engage in the practice of massage therapy and holding oneself out or designating oneself to the public as a massage therapist or massage establishment. The practice of massage therapy shall include effleurage (stroking), petrissage (kneading), tapotement (percussion), compression, vibration, friction (active/passive range of motion), stretching activities as they pertain to massage therapy, Shiatsu, acupressure, reflexology, and Swedish massage either by hand, forearm, elbow, foot, or with mechanical appliances for the purpose of body massage. Massage therapy may include the use of lubricants such as salts, powders, liquids, creams with the exception of prescriptive or medicinal creams, heat lamps, hot and cold stones, whirlpool, hot and cold packs, salt glow, body wraps, or steam cabinet baths. It shall not include electrotherapy, laser therapy, microwave, colonic therapy, injection therapy, or manipulation of the joints. Equivalent terms for massage therapy are massage, therapeutic massage, massage technology, body work, or any derivation of those terms. As used in this Chapter, the terms "therapy" and "therapeutic" shall not include diagnosis, the treatment of illness or disease, or any service or procedure for which a license to practice medicine, chiropractic, physical therapy, or podiatry is required by law.

3553. Application of Chapter; exceptions and exemptions
C. Nothing in this Chapter shall be construed as preventing or restricting the practice of any person licensed or certified in this state under any other law from engaging in the profession or occupation for which he is licensed or certified.

Louisiana Licensed Professional Counselors Board of Exmainers
8631 Summa Avenue
Baton Rouge LA 70809
(225) 765-2515
Fax: (225) 765-2514
lpcboard@eatel.net

503. Definitions for Licensed Professional Counselors A. For purposes of this rule, the following definitions will apply:
Licensed Professional Counselor—any person who holds oneself out to the public for a fee or other personal gain, by any title or description of services incorporating the words "licensed professional counselor" or any similar term, and who offers to render professional mental health counseling/psychotherapy services denoting a client counselor relationship in which the counselor assumes the responsibility for knowledge, skill, and ethical consideration needed to assist individuals, groups, organizations, or the general public, and who implies that he/she is licensed to practice mental health counseling. Mental Health Counseling/Psychotherapy Services— rendering or offering prevention, assessment, diagnosis, and treatment, which includes psychotherapy of mental, emotional, behavioral, and addiction disorders to individuals, groups, organizations, or the general public by a licensed professional counselor which is consistent with his professional training as prescribed by R.S. 37:1107(A)(8), and code of ethics/behavior involving the application of principles, methods, or procedures of the mental health counseling profession. However, nothing in this Chapter shall be construed to authorize any person licensed hereunder to administer or interpret tests in accordance with the provision of R.S.37:2352(5), except as provided by LAC 46:LXIII.1702.E, or engage in the practice of psychology or to prescribe, either orally or in writing, distribute, dispense, or administer any medications. Practice of Mental Health

Laws Governing Energy Medicine Practitioners

Counseling/Psychotherapy— rendering or offering prevention, assessment, diagnosis, and treatment, which includes psychotherapy of mental, emotional, behavioral, and addiction disorders to individuals, groups, organizations, or the general public by a licensed professional counselor, which is consistent with his professional training as prescribed by R.S. 37:1107(A)(8), and code of ethics/behavior involving the application of principles, methods, or procedures of the mental health counseling profession which includes but is not limited to: a. Mental Health Counseling/Psychotherapy— assisting an individual or group through psychotherapy by rendering or offering prevention, assessment, diagnosis, and treatment, which includes psychotherapy of mental, emotional, behavioral, and addiction disorders. This professional relationship empowers diverse individuals, PROFESSIONAL AND OCCUPATIONAL STANDARDS Louisiana Administrative Code July 2013 4 families, and groups to accomplish mental health, wellness, education, and career goals

Chapter 17. Exclusions for Licensed Professional Counselors §1701. Scope A. The following persons and their activities are exempted from the licensing requirements of R.S. 37:1101-1122 and these rules.

D. Any persons licensed, certified, or registered under any other provision of the state law, as long as the services rendered are consistent with their laws, professional training, and code of ethics, provided they do not represent themselves as licensed professional counselors or mental health counselors, unless they have also been licensed under the provisions of R.S. 37:1107. E. Any priest, rabbi, Christian Science practitioner, or minister of the gospel of any religious denomination, provided they are practicing within the employment of their church or religious affiliated institution and they do not represent themselves as licensed professional counselors or mental health counselors unless they have also been licensed under the provisions of R.S. 37:1107.

Maine

State of Maine Professional & Financial Regulation
Office of Professional and Occupational Regulation
Massage Therapy Licensure
35 State House Station
Augusta Maine 04333-0035
207-624-8603
www.maine.gov/pfr/professionallicensing

14301. Definitions
   3. Massage therapy. "Massage therapy" means a scientific or skillful manipulation of soft tissue for therapeutic or remedial purposes, specifically for improving muscle tone and circulation and promoting health and physical well-being. The term includes, but is not limited to, manual and mechanical procedures for the purpose of treating soft tissue only, the use of supplementary aids such as rubbing alcohol, liniments, oils, antiseptics, powders, herbal preparations, creams or lotions, procedures or preparations commonly used in this practice. This term specifically excludes manipulation of the spine or articulations and excludes sexual contact as defined in Title 17-A, section 251, subsection 1, paragraph D.

14307. Exemptions to registration or certification
   1. Other professionals. This chapter does not apply to the activities or services of members of other professions licensed, certified or registered by the State, including, but not limited to, physicians, chiropractors, physical therapists, cosmetologists or registered nurses performing soft tissue manipulation consistent with the laws of the State governing their practices, provided they do not use the title "massage therapist" or "massage practitioner."

[1993, c. 245, §8 (AMD).]
   2. Other exemptions. This chapter does not apply to the activities and services of individuals who practice other forms of tissue work exclusive of massage therapy,

such as rolfing, Trager, reflexology, Shiatsu, Reiki and polarity, if those practitioners do not use the title "massage therapist" or "massage practitioner," unless they choose to meet the requirements of this chapter.

State of Maine Professional & Financial Regulation
Office of Professional and Occupational Regulation
Counseling Professionals Licensure
35 State House Station
Augusta Maine 04333-0035
207-624-8603
www.maine.gov/pfr/professionallicensing

Title 32: Professions and Occupations
Chapter 119: Counseling Professionals
13851. Definitions
7-A. Pastoral counselor. "Pastoral counselor" means an individual who is trained and certified to provide for a fee, monetary or otherwise, pastoral counseling, which is ministry to individuals, Families, couples, groups, organizations and the general public involving the application of principles and procedures of counseling to assess and treat intrapersonal and interpersonal problems and other dysfunctional behavior of a social and spiritual nature, and to assist in the overall development and healing process of those served.
8. Procedures of counseling. "Procedures of counseling" means methods and techniques that include, but are not limited to, the following.
A. "Assessment" means selecting, administering, and interpreting instruments designed to assess personal, interpersonal, and group characteristics. [1989, c. 465, §3 (NEW).]
B. "Consulting" means the application of scientific principles and procedures in counseling to provide assistance in understanding and solving a current or potential problem that the client may have in relation to a 3rd party, be it an individual, a family, a group or an organization. [1989, c.465, §3 (NEW).]
D. "Referral" means the evaluation of information to identify needs or problems of the counselee and to determine the advisability of referral to other specialists,

informing the counselee of that judgment, and communicating as requested or deemed appropriate with referral sources.

9. Professional counselor. "Professional counselor" means a person who, for a fee, monetary or otherwise, renders or offers to render to individuals, families, groups, organizations or the general public a service involving the application of principles and procedures of counseling to assist those served in achieving more effective personal, emotional, social, educational and vocational development and adjustment.

Maryland

Maryland Department of Health and Mental Hygiene
Board of Chiropractic & Massage Therapy Examiners
Metro Executive Building
4201 Patterson Avenue, Suite 301
Baltimore MD 21215-2299
:410-764-4738
http://dhmh.maryland.gov/massage

10.43.17.02. 02 Definitions.
(6) Massage Therapy.
(a) "Massage therapy" means the use of manual techniques on soft tissues of the human body including effleurage (stroking), petrissage (kneading), tapotement (tapping), stretching, compression, vibration, and friction.
(b) "Massage therapy" includes massage, myotherapy, and synonyms or derivatives of these terms
(c) "Massage therapy" does not include the:
(iii) Laying on of hands, consisting of pressure or movement, with the exception of such techniques described in §B(6)(a) of this regulation on a fully clothed individual to specifically affect the electromagnetic energy or energetic field of the human body.

Maryland Department of Health and Mental Hygiene
Board of Professional Counselors
4201 Patterson Avenue
Baltimore, Maryland 21215-2299
Phone: 410-764-4732
Fax: 410-358-1610
http://dhmh.maryland.gov/bop

Health Occupation Article – Title 17. Professional Counselors and Therapists
Subtitle 1. Definitions; General Provisions
17-101. Definitions

(1) To develop understanding of intrapersonal and interpersonal problems;
(2) To define goals;
(3) To make decisions
(4) To plan a course of action reflecting the needs, interests, abilities of the individual, family, or group, and
(5) To use informational and community resources, as these procedures are related to personal, social, emotional, educational, and vocational development and adjustment

17-103. Practices not affected by title.
This title foes not limit the right of an individual to practice a health occupation that the individual is authorized to practice under this article.

Massachusetts

Massachusetts Consumer Affairs and Business Regulation
Board of Registration of Massage Therapy
1000 Washington Street, Suite 710
Boston, Massachusetts 02118-6100
(617) 727-3074
Fax: (617) 727-1944
http://www.mass.gov/ocabr/licensee/dpl-boards

269 CMR 2.00: Definitions
Massage: The systematic treatment of the soft tissues of the body by use of pressure, friction, stroking, percussion, kneading, vibration by manual or mechanical means, range of motion for purposes of demonstrating muscle excursion or muscle flexibility and nonspecific stretching. Massage therapy may include the use of oil, ice, hot and cold packs, tub, shower, steam, dry heat or cabinet baths, in which the primary intent is to enhance or restore the health and well-being of the client. Massage therapy shall not include diagnoses of illness or disease, the prescribing of drugs or medicines, high-velocity, low amplitude thrust applied to the joint, electrical stimulation, application of ultrasound, exercise, spinal or other joint manipulations or any services or procedures for which a license to practice medicine, chiropractic, occupational therapy, physical therapy or podiatry is required by law. Massage Therapy also shall not include the practice of a person who uses touch, words or directed movement to deepen awareness of the patterns of movement in the body, or the affectation of the human energy system or acupoints or Qi meridians of the human body while engaged within the scope of practice of a profession with established standards and ethics, including, but not limited to, the Feldenkrais Method, Reflexology, The Trager Approach, Ayurvedic Therapies, Rolf Structural Integration, Polarity or Polarity Therapy, Polarity Therapy Bodywork, Asian Bodywork Therapy that does not constitute Massage as defined in M.G.L. c. 135, Acupressure, Jin Shin Do, Qi Gong, Tui Na, Shiatsu, Body-mind Centering and Reiki. For purposes of 269 CMR et seq., the use of the term "Massage" shall also mean the term "Massage therapy".

Massachusetts Consumer Affairs and Business Regulation
Board of Registration of Allied Mental Health and Human Services Professions

1000 Washington Street, Suite 710
Boston, Massachusetts 02118-6100
Phone: (617) 727-3074
Fax: (617) 727-1944
www.mass.gov/ocabr/license

262 CMR 2.00: Requirements For Licensure As a Mental Health Counselor
- *2.02: Definitions*

Mental Health Counseling. The rendering of professional services to individuals, families or groups for compensation, monetary or otherwise. These professional services include: applying the principles, methods, and theories of counseling, human development, learning theory, group and family dynamics, the etiology of mental illness and dysfunctional behavior and psychotherapeutic techniques to define goals and develop a treatment plan of action aimed toward the prevention, treatment and resolution of mental and emotional dysfunction and intra or interpersonal disorders to all persons irrespective of diagnosis. The practice of mental health counseling includes, but is not limited to, assessment, diagnosis and treatment, counseling and psychotherapy, of a nonmedical nature of mental and emotional disorders, psychoeducational techniques aimed at prevention of such disorders, and consultation to individuals, couples, families, groups, organizations and communities.

Michigan

Michigan Board of Massage Therapy
Department of Licensing and Regulatory Affairs
PO Box 30670
Lansing, MI 48909
(517) 335-0918
Fax: (517) 373-2179
bhpinfo@michigan.gov
http://www.michigan.gov/lara

PUBLIC HEALTH CODE (EXCERPT)
Act 368 of 1978
333.17951 Definitions.
(a) "Feldenkrais method" means a system of somatic education in which touch and words are used to eliminate faulty habits, learn new patterns of self-organization and action, and improve a person's own functional movement patterns. Feldenkrais method is based on principles of physics, biomechanics, and an understanding of, or learning about, human development.
(c) "Polarity therapy" means diverse applications affecting the human energy system and includes energetic approaches to somatic contact, verbal facilitation, nutrition, exercise, and health education. Polarity therapy does not make medical claims, diagnose physical ailments, or allow prescription of medications.
(d) "Practice of massage therapy" means the application of a system of structured touch, pressure, movement, and holding to the soft tissue of the human body in which the primary intent is to enhance or restore the health and well-being of the client. Practice of massage therapy includes complementary methods, including the external application of water, heat, cold, lubrication, salt scrubs, body wraps, or other topical preparations; and electromechanical devices that mimic or enhance the actions possible by the hands. Practice of massage therapy does not include medical diagnosis; practice of physical therapy; high-velocity, low-amplitude thrust to a joint; electrical stimulation; application of ultrasound; or prescription of medicines.

(f) "Trager approach" means a form of movement education that uses subtle directed movements and the skilled touch of a practitioner. The Trager approach combines physical movement with sensory awareness and internal imagery designed to increase the client's self-awareness and generate physiological changes in the body tissues so as to allow the client to experience a new way of moving his or her body.

333.17957 Massage therapy; license required; exceptions.
Sec. 17957.
(1) An individual shall not engage in the practice of massage therapy unless licensed under this part. The practices for which a license is not required under this subsection include, but are not limited to, all of the following:
(a) The use of touch, words, or directed movement to deepen awareness of patterns of movement in the body as long as those services are not designated or implied to be massage or massage therapy. These practices include, but are not limited to, all of the following:
(i) The Feldenkrais method.
(ii) The Trager approach.
(b) The affectation of the human energy system or acupoints or qi meridians of the human body while engaged within the scope of practice of a profession with established standards and ethics and as long as those services are not designated or implied to be massage or massage therapy. These practices include, but are not limited to, all of the following:
(i) Polarity or polarity therapy.
(ii) Asian bodywork therapy.
(iii) Reiki.
(iv) Shiatsu.
(c) Reflex
(1) An individual shall not engage in the practice of massage therapy unless licensed under this part. The practices for which a license is not required under this subsection include, but are not limited to, all of the following:
(a) The use of touch, words, or directed movement to deepen awareness of patterns of movement in the body as long as those services are not designated or implied to

be massage or massage therapy. These practices include, but are not limited to, all of the following:
(i) The Feldenkrais method.
(ii) The Trager approach.
(b) The affectation of the human energy system or acupoints or qi meridians of the human body while engaged within the scope of practice of a profession with established standards and ethics and as long as those services are not designated or implied to be massage or massage therapy. These practices include, but are not limited to, all of the following:
(i) Polarity or polarity therapy.
(ii) Asian bodywork therapy.
(iii) Reiki.
(iv) Shiatsu.
(c) Reflexology.

Michigan Department of Licensing and Regulatory Affairs
Bureau of Health Care Services
Board of Counseling
PO Box 30670
Lansing MI 48909
(517) 335-0918
www.michigan.gov/healthlicense

PUBLIC HEALTH CODE (EXCERPT)
Act 368 of 1978
Part 181
COUNSELING
333.18101 Definitions.
Sec. 18101.
As used in this part:
(a) "Counseling principles, methods, or procedures" means a developmental approach that systematically assists an individual through the application of any of the following procedures:

(i) Evaluation and appraisal techniques. As used in this subparagraph, "appraisal techniques" means selecting, administering, scoring, and interpreting instruments and procedures designed to assess an individual's aptitudes, interests, attitudes, abilities, achievements, and personal characteristics for developmental purposes and not for psychodiagnostic purposes.
(ii) Exploring alternative solutions.
(iii) Developing and providing a counseling plan for mental and emotional development.
(iv) Guidance.
(v) Psychoeducational consulting.
(vi) Learning theory.
(vii) Individual and group techniques emphasizing prevention.
(viii) Counseling techniques.
(ix) Behavioral modification techniques.
(d) "Practice of counseling" or "counseling" means the rendering to individuals, groups, families, organizations, or the general public a service involving the application of clinical counseling principles, methods, or procedures for the purpose of achieving social, personal, career, and emotional development and with the goal of promoting and enhancing healthy self actualizing and satisfying lifestyles whether the services are rendered in an educational, business, health, private practice, or human services setting. The practice of counseling does not include the practice of psychology except for those preventive techniques, counseling techniques, or behavior modification techniques for which the licensed professional counselor or limited licensed counselor has been specifically trained. The practice of counseling does not include the practice of medicine such as prescribing drugs or administering electroconvulsive therapy. A counselor shall not hold himself or herself out as a psychologist as defined in section 18201. A counselor shall not hold himself or herself out as a marriage and family counselor providing marriage counseling pursuant to section 1501 of the occupational code, Act No. 299 of the Public Acts of 1980, being section 339.1501 of the Michigan Compiled Laws.

Minnesota

Minnesota has no massage board or regulations at the time of this writing. The Minnesota chapter of the American Massage Therapy Association, www.amtamn.org, can answer some questions.
Minnesota does have rules concerning complimentary and alternative health care practices.

Office of Complimentary and Alternative Health Care Practitioners
PO Box 64882
St Paul MN 55164-0882
651-201-3721
Health.HOP@state.mn.us
http://www.health.state.mn.us/

Chapter 146A. Complementary and Alternative Health Care Practices
146A.01 DEFINITIONS.
   Subd. 3. Complementary and alternative health care client.

"Complementary and alternative health care client" means an individual who receives services from an unlicensed complementary and alternative health care practitioner.
   Subd. 4. Complementary and alternative health care practices.

(a) "Complementary and alternative health care practices" means the broad domain of complementary and alternative healing methods and treatments, including but not limited to: (1) acupressure; (2) anthroposophy; (3) aroma therapy; (4) ayurveda; (5) cranial sacral therapy; (6) culturally traditional healing practices; (7) detoxification practices and therapies; (8) energetic healing; (9) polarity therapy; (10) folk practices; (11) healing practices utilizing food, food supplements, nutrients, and the physical forces of heat, cold, water, touch, and light; (12) Gerson therapy and colostrum therapy; (13) healing touch; (14) herbology or herbalism; (15) homeopathy; (16) nondiagnostic iridology; (17) body work, massage, and massage therapy; (18) meditation; (19) mind-body healing practices; (20) naturopathy; (21) noninvasive instrumentalities; and (22) traditional Oriental practices, such as Qi Gong energy healing.

Subd. 6. *Unlicensed complementary and alternative health care practitioner.*

"Unlicensed complementary and alternative health care practitioner" means a person who:

(1) either:

(i) is not licensed or registered by a health-related licensing board or the commissioner of health; or

(ii) is licensed or registered by the commissioner of health or a health-related licensing board other than the Board of Medical Practice, the Board of Dentistry, the Board of Chiropractic Examiners, or the Board of Podiatric Medicine, but does not hold oneself out to the public as being licensed or registered by the commissioner or a health-related licensing board when engaging in complementary and alternative health care;

(2) has not had a license or registration issued by a health-related licensing board or the commissioner of health revoked or has not been disciplined in any manner at any time in the past, unless the right to engage in complementary and alternative health care practices has been established by order of the commissioner of health;

(3) is engaging in complementary and alternative health care practices; and

(4) is providing complementary and alternative health care services for remuneration or is holding oneself out to the public as a practitioner of complementary and alternative health care practices.

146A.065 COMPLEMENTARY AND ALTERNATIVE HEALTH CARE PRACTICES BY LICENSED OR REGISTERED HEALTH CARE PRACTITIONERS.

(a) A health care practitioner licensed or registered by the commissioner or a health-related licensing board, who engages in complementary and alternative health care while practicing under the practitioner's license or registration, shall be regulated by and be under the jurisdiction of the applicable health-related licensing board with regard to the complementary and alternative health care practices.

(b) A health care practitioner licensed or registered by the commissioner or a health-related licensing board shall not be subject to disciplinary action solely on the basis of utilizing complementary and alternative health care practices as defined in section 146A.01, subdivision 4, paragraph (a), as a component of a patient's treatment, or for referring a patient to a complementary and alternative health care practitioner as defined in section 146A.01, subdivision 6.

(c) A health care practitioner licensed or registered by the commissioner or a health-related licensing board who utilizes complementary and alternative health care practices must provide patients receiving these services with a written copy of the complementary and alternative health care client bill of rights pursuant to section 146A.11.

(d) Nothing in this section shall be construed to prohibit or restrict the commissioner or a health-related licensing board from imposing disciplinary action for conduct that violates provisions of the applicable licensed or registered health care practitioner's practice act.

146A.11 COMPLEMENTARY AND ALTERNATIVE HEALTH CARE CLIENT BILL OF RIGHTS.

Subdivision 1. Scope.

(a) All unlicensed complementary and alternative health care practitioners shall provide to each complementary and alternative health care client prior to providing treatment a written copy of the complementary and alternative health care client bill of rights. A copy must also be posted in a prominent location in the office of the unlicensed complementary and alternative health care practitioner. Reasonable accommodations shall be made for those clients who cannot read or who have communication disabilities and those who do not read or speak English. The complementary and alternative health care client bill of rights shall include the following:

(1) the name, complementary and alternative health care title, business address, and telephone number of the unlicensed complementary and alternative health care practitioner;

(2) the degrees, training, experience, or other qualifications of the practitioner regarding the complementary and alternative health care being provided, followed by the following statement in bold print:

"THE STATE OF MINNESOTA HAS NOT ADOPTED ANY EDUCATIONAL AND TRAINING STANDARDS FOR UNLICENSED COMPLEMENTARY AND ALTERNATIVE HEALTH CARE PRACTITIONERS. THIS STATEMENT OF CREDENTIALS IS FOR INFORMATION PURPOSES ONLY.

Under Minnesota law, an unlicensed complementary and alternative health care practitioner may not provide a medical diagnosis or recommend discontinuance of medically prescribed treatments. If a client desires a diagnosis from a licensed physician, chiropractor, or acupuncture practitioner, or services from a physician, chiropractor, nurse, osteopath, physical therapist, dietitian, nutritionist, acupuncture practitioner, athletic trainer, or any other type of health care provider, the client may seek such services at any time.";

(3) the name, business address, and telephone number of the practitioner's supervisor, if any;

(4) notice that a complementary and alternative health care client has the right to file a complaint with the practitioner's supervisor, if any, and the procedure for filing complaints;

(5) the name, address, and telephone number of the office of unlicensed complementary and alternative health care practice and notice that a client may file complaints with the office;

(6) the practitioner's fees per unit of service, the practitioner's method of billing for such fees, the names of any insurance companies that have agreed to reimburse the practitioner, or health maintenance organizations with whom the practitioner contracts to provide service, whether the practitioner accepts Medicare, medical assistance, or general assistance medical care, and whether the practitioner is willing to accept partial payment, or to waive payment, and in what circumstances;

(7) a statement that the client has a right to reasonable notice of changes in services or charges;

(8) a brief summary, in plain language, of the theoretical approach used by the practitioner in providing services to clients;

(9) notice that the client has a right to complete and current information concerning the practitioner's assessment and recommended service that is to be provided, including the expected duration of the service to be provided;

(10) a statement that clients may expect courteous treatment and to be free from verbal, physical, or sexual abuse by the practitioner;

(11) a statement that client records and transactions with the practitioner are confidential, unless release of these records is authorized in writing by the client, or otherwise provided by law;

(12) a statement of the client's right to be allowed access to records and written information from records in accordance with sections 144.291 to 144.298;

(13) a statement that other services may be available in the community, including where information concerning services is available;

(14) a statement that the client has the right to choose freely among available practitioners and to change practitioners after services have begun, within the limits of health insurance, medical assistance, or other health programs;

(15) a statement that the client has a right to coordinated transfer when there will be a change in the provider of services;

(16) a statement that the client may refuse services or treatment, unless otherwise provided by law; and

(17) a statement that the client may assert the client's rights without retaliation.

(b) This section does not apply to an unlicensed complementary and alternative health care practitioner who is employed by or is a volunteer in a hospital or hospice who provides services to a client in a hospital or under an appropriate hospice plan of care. Patients receiving complementary and alternative health care services in an inpatient hospital or under an appropriate hospice plan of care shall have and be made aware of the right to file a complaint with the hospital or hospice provider through which the practitioner is employed or registered as a volunteer.

(c) This section does not apply to a health care practitioner licensed or registered by the commissioner of health or a health-related licensing board who utilizes complementary and alternative health care practices within the scope of practice of the health care practitioner's professional license.

Subd. 2. Acknowledgment by client.

Prior to the provision of any service, a complementary and alternative health care client must sign a written statement attesting that the client has received the complementary and alternative health care client bill of rights.

Minnesota Board of BOARD OF BEHAVIORAL HEALTH AND THERAPY
Licensed Professional Counselor (LPC)
St Paul MN
651) 201-2760
Contact Info: patricia.labrocca@state.mn.us
http://mn.gov/elicense/licenses/licensedetail

I found lots of information about various issues concerning counseling but no definition of counselor or counseling. I found the following about informed consent interesting.

2150.7505 DEFINITIONS.
   Subp. 13.

Informed consent.
   "Informed consent" means an agreement between a provider and a client that authorizes the provider to engage in a professional activity affecting the client. Informed consent requires that the client be given sufficient information to decide knowingly whether to agree to the proposed professional activity, that the information be discussed in language that the client can reasonably be expected to understand, and that the consent be given without undue influence by the provider.

Mississippi

Mississippi State Board of Massage Therapy
PO Box 20
Morton, MS 39117
Phone: 601.732.6038
Email: director@msbmt.state.ms.us
http://www.msbmt.state.ms.us/

The following is no longer valid as it has been repealed. I found no replacement for the repealed definitions. I have included it only because it gives the spirit of the state requirements, not the actual laws. The exemption definition is quite vague.

Source: Miss Code Ann. § 73-67-9 (Rev. 2008); § 73-67-15 (Rev. 2008); 73-67-17 (Rev. 2008) Repealed July 1, 2013
Rule 1.4. Definitions
K. "Massage" means touch, stroking, kneading, stretching, friction, percussion and vibration, and includes holding, positioning, causing movement of the soft tissues and applying manual touch and pressure to the body (excluding an osseous tissue manipulation or adjustment). "Therapy" means action aimed at achieving or increasing health and wellness. "Massage therapy" means the profession in which the practitioner applies massage techniques with the intent of positively affecting the health and wellbeing of the client, and may adjunctively (i) apply allied modalities, heat, cold, water and topical preparations not classified as prescription drugs, (ii) use hand held tools such as electrical hand massagers used adjunctively to the application of hand massage or devices designed as t-bars or knobbies, and (iii) instruct self care and stress management. "Manual" means by use of hand or body.
Rule 7.2 Exemption From Licensure A. The provisions of this chapter regarding licensure do not apply to the following:
1. Persons state licensed, state registered, state certified, or otherwise s state credentialed by the laws of this State to include massage therapy as part of their practice,

or other allied modalities that are certified by a nationally accredited organization recognized by the Board;
2. Students enrolled in a massage therapy school and at the same time working in a student clinic; and out of state massage therapy instructors when teaching in these programs. July 1, 2011 Page 28
B. Any exemption granted under this section is effective only insofar as and to the extent that the bona fide practice of the profession or business of the person exempted overlaps into the field comprehended by this law, and exemptions under this section are only for those activities that are currently authorized in the course of bona fide practice of the business or profession of the person exempted.

Mississippi State Board of Examiners for Licensed Professional Counselors
239 North Lamar Street
Suite 402
Jackson, MS 39201
Office: 601 359-1010
Fax: 601 359-1030
www.lpc.ms.gov/boardinformation

Rules and Regulations Mississippi State Board of Examiners for Licensed Professional Counselors
Rule 1.4: Definitions. Note: The terms counseling and psychotherapy are used interchangeably throughout this document.
J. Counseling/Psychotherapy Procedures: Counseling/Psychotherapy is the application of mental health, psychological, or human development principles, through cognitive, affective, behavioral, or systemic intervention strategies that address wellness, personal growth, or career development, as well as pathology. Counseling/Psychotherapy involves diagnosis, assessment, and treatment by the use of counseling/psychotherapy methods and techniques, both verbal and 5 nonverbal, which require the application of principles, methods, or procedures of understanding, predicting and/or influencing behavior and motivation; the use of informational and community resources for personal or social development; the use of group and/or placement methods and techniques which serve to further the goals of counseling/

psychotherapy; designing, conducting and interpreting research on human subjects and on any consultation on any item above; appraisal techniques including, but not limited to, testing of achievement, abilities, interests, aptitudes and personality.
S. Practice of Counseling/Psychotherapy: Rendering, offering to render, or supervising those who render to individuals, group organizations, corporations, institutions, government agencies, or the general public any service involving the application of counseling procedures (See Chapter 1, Section 4, H., p.4) and other related areas of behavioral sciences to help in learning how to solve problems or make decisions related to personal growth, marriage, family, or other interpersonal or intrapersonal concerns.

Missouri

Missouri Board of Therapeutic Massage
3605 Missouri Boulevard
P.O. Box 1335
Jefferson City, MO 65102-1335
573.522.6277
573.751.0735 Fax
massagether@pr.mo.gov
http://pr.mo.gov/massage.asp

Missouri Revised Statutes
Chapter 324
Occupations and Professions General Provisions

Section 324.240.1
324.240. As used in sections 324.240 to 324.275, the following terms shall mean:
(7) "Massage therapy", a health care profession which involves the treatment of the body's tonus system through the scientific or skillful touching, rubbing, pressing or other movements of the soft tissues of the body with the hands, forearms, elbows, or feet, or with the aid of mechanical apparatus, for relaxation, therapeutic, remedial or health maintenance purposes to enhance the mental and physical well-being of the client, but does not include the prescription of medication, spinal or joint manipulation, the diagnosis of illness or disease, or any service or procedure for which a license to practice medicine, chiropractic, physical therapy, or podiatry is required by law, or to those occupations defined in chapter 329;
324.265.
7. The following practitioners are exempt from the provisions of this section upon filing written proof with the board that they meet one or more of the following:
   (2) Persons who restrict their manipulation of the soft tissues of the human body to the hands, feet or ears;
   (3) Persons who use touch and words to deepen awareness of existing patterns of movement in the human body as well as to suggest new possibilities of movement;

Laws Governing Energy Medicine Practitioners

(4) Persons who manipulate the human body above the neck, below the elbow, and below the knee and do not disrobe the client in performing such manipulation.

Committee for Professional Counselors
3605 Missouri Boulevard
P.O. Box 1335
Jefferson City, MO 65102-1335
573.751.0018
573.751.0735 Fax
profcounselor@pr.mo.gov
http://pr.mo.gov/counselors.asp

Missouri Revised Statutes
Chapter 337

Psychologists--Professional Counselors--Social Workers Section 337.500.1 *Definitions.*
337.500. As used in sections 337.500 to 337.540, unless the context clearly requires otherwise, the following words and phrases mean:

(6) "Practice of professional counseling", rendering, offering to render, or supervising those who render to individuals, couples, groups, organizations, institutions, corporations, schools, government agencies, or the general public any counseling service involving the application of counseling procedures, and the principles and methods thereof, to assist in achieving more effective intrapersonal or interpersonal, marital, decisional, social, educational, vocational, developmental, or rehabilitative adjustments;

(7) "Professional counseling", includes, but is not limited to:

(a) The use of verbal or nonverbal counseling or both techniques, methods, or procedures based on principles for assessing, understanding, or influencing behavior (such as principles of learning, conditioning, perception, motivation, thinking, emotions, or social systems);

(b) Appraisal or assessment, which means selecting, administering, scoring, or interpreting instruments designed to assess a person's or group's aptitudes, intelligence, attitudes, abilities, achievement, interests, and personal characteristics;

(c) The use of referral or placement techniques or both which serve to further the goals of counseling;

(d) Therapeutic vocational or personal or both rehabilitation in relation to coping with or adapting to physical disability, emotional disability, or intellectual disability or any combination of the three;

(e) Designing, conducting, and interpreting research;

(f) The use of group methods or techniques to promote the goals of counseling;

(g) The use of informational and community resources for career, personal, or social development;

(h) Consultation on any item in paragraphs (a) through (g) above; and

(i) No provision of sections 337.500 to 337.540, or of chapter 354 or 375, shall be construed to mandate benefits or third-party reimbursement for services of professional counselors in the policies or contracts of any insurance company, health services corporation or other third-party payer

Montana

Board of Licensed Massage Therapists
301 South Park, 4th Floor (map)
P.O. Box 200513
Helena, MT 59620-0513
Fax: (406) 841-2305
dlibsdlmt@mt.gov
www.massagetherapists.mt.gov

Montana Code Annotated 2014
37-33-403. Definitions. As used in this chapter, the following definitions apply:
(4) (a) (i) "Massage therapy" when provided by a massage therapist means the application of a system of structured touch, pressure, positioning, or holding to soft tissues of the body, Swedish massage, effleurage, petrissage, tapotement, percussion, friction, vibration, compression, passive and active stretching or movement within the normal anatomical range of motion, the external application of water, heat, cold, lubricants, salts, skin brushing, or other topical preparations not classified as prescription drugs, providing information for self-care stress management, and the determination of whether massage is contraindicated and whether referral to another health care practitioner is recommended.

(ii) The techniques described in subsection (4)(a)(i) must be applied by the massage therapist through the use of hands, forearms, elbows, knees, or feet or through the use of hand-held tools that mimic or support the action of the hands and are primarily intended to enhance or restore health and well-being by promoting pain relief, stress reduction, and relaxation.

(b) The term does not include providing examinations for the purpose of diagnosis, providing treatments that are outside the scope of massage therapy, attempts to adjust, manipulate, or mobilize any articulations of the body or spine by the use of high-velocity, low-amplitude thrusting force, exercise, exercise instruction or prescription, or the use of tape when applied to restrict joint movement, manual or mechanical traction when applied to the spine or extremities for the purposes of joint mobilization or manipulation, injection therapy, laser

therapy, microwave diathermy, electrical stimulation, ultrasound, iontophoresis, or phonophoresis.

37-33-404. Exemptions -- rules. *(1) The provisions of this chapter do not limit or regulate the scope of practice of any other profession licensed under the laws of this state, including but not limited to medicine, dentistry, osteopathy, podiatry, nursing, physical therapy, chiropractic, acupuncture, veterinary medicine, occupational therapy, naturopathic medicine, cosmetology, manicuring, barbering, esthetics, electrology, professional counseling, social work, psychology, or athletic training.*
(4) The provisions of this chapter do not limit or regulate the practice of Native American traditional healing or faith healing.
(5) (a) The provisions of this chapter do not limit or regulate the practice of any person who uses:

(i) touch, words, and directed movement to deepen awareness of existing patterns of movement in the body, as well as to suggest new possibilities of movement. Exempt practices under this subsection (5)(a)(i) include but are not limited to the Feldenkrais method of somatic education, the Trager approach to movement education, and body-mind centering.

(ii) touch to affect the human energy systems, energy meridians, or energy fields. Exempted practices under this subsection (5)(a)(ii) include but are not limited to polarity bodywork therapy, Asian bodywork therapy, acupressure, jin shin do, qigong, reiki, shiatsu, and tui na.

(iii) touch to effect change on the integration of the structure of the physical body. Exempt practices under this subsection (5)(a)(iii) include but are not limited to the Rolf method of structural integration, Rolfing, and Hellerwork.

(iv) touch to affect the reflex areas located in the hands, feet, and outer ears. Exempt practices under this subsection (5)(a)(iv) include but are not limited to reflexology.

(b) The exemptions in subsection (5)(a) apply only if:

(i) the person is recognized by or meets the established requirements of either a professional organization or credentialing agency that represents or certifies the respective practice based on a minimum level of training, demonstration of competence, and adherence to ethical standards; and

(ii) the person's services are not designated as or implied to be massage therapy.

Board of Social Work Examiners & Professional Counselors & Therapists
301 South Park, 4th Floor
P.O. Box 200513
Helena, MT 59620-0513
Fax: (406) 841-2305
dlibsdswpc@mt.gov
www.swpc.mt.gov

Rule: 24.219.301
24.219.301 DEFINITIONS
(1) "Direct client contact" means physical presence, telephonic presence, or interactive video link presence of the client, client family member, or client representative.

(5) "Psychosocial methods" means those professional techniques which are identified as clinical in nature and:
(a) enhance the problem solving and coping capacity of people;
(b) link people with systems that provide them with resources, services, and opportunities;
(c) promote effective and humane operation of these systems; and
(d) contribute to the development and improvement of social policy.

(6) "Psychotherapy and counseling" means the therapeutic process of:
(a) conducting assessments and diagnoses for the purpose of establishing treatment goals and objectives; or
(b) planning, implementing, and evaluating treatment plans that use treatment interventions to facilitate human development and to identify and remediate mental, emotional or behavioral disorders and associated distresses that interfere with mental health.

Nebraska

Office of Behavioral Health & Consumer Services
Nebraska State Office Building
301 Centennial Mall South
14th and M Streets
1st Floor
Lincoln, Nebraska
(402) 471-2117
rita.watson@nebraska.gov
http://dhhs.ne.gov/publichealth

STATUTES PERTAINING TO THE MASSAGE THERAPY PRACTICE ACT
38-1706. *Massage therapy, defined.* Massage therapy means the physical, mechanical, or electrical manipulation of soft tissue for the therapeutic purposes of enhancing muscle relaxation, reducing stress, improving circulation, or instilling a greater sense of well-being and may include the use of oil, salt glows, heat lamps, and hydrotherapy. Massage therapy does not include diagnosis or treatment or use of procedures for which a license to practice medicine or surgery, chiropractic, or podiatry is required nor the use of microwave diathermy, shortwave diathermy, ultrasound, transcutaneous electrical nerve stimulation, electrical stimulation of over thirty-five volts, neurological hyperstimulation, or spinal and joint adjustments. Source: Laws 2007, LB463, § 613. Operative date December 1, 2008.

38-1708. *Massage therapy; persons excepted.* The Massage Therapy Practice Act shall not be construed to include the following classes of persons: (1) Licensed physicians and surgeons, osteopathic physicians, chiropractors, registered nurses, practical nurses, cosmetologists, estheticians, nail technicians, physical therapists, barbers, and other persons credentialed under the Uniform Credentialing Act who are exclusively engaged in the practice of their respective professions;

Nebraska Department of Health and Human Services - Division of Public Health
Board of Mental Health
Nebraska State Office Building
301 Centennial Mall South
14th and M Streets
1st Floor
Lincoln, Nebraska
(402) 471-2115

94-002 DEFINITIONS
Counseling means a professional relationship in which a mental health practitioner assists another (client) to understand, cope with, solve, and/or prevent problems, such as, but not limited to areas of education, vocation, and/or interpersonal relationships in the social environment.

Professional Counseling means the assessment and treatment of mental and emotional disorders within the context of professional counseling theory and practice of individuals, couples, families, or groups for remuneration and includes, but is not limited to:

1. Assisting individuals or groups through the counseling relationship to develop understanding, define goals, plan action, and change behavior with the goal of reflecting interests, abilities, aptitudes, and needs as they are related to personal and social concerns, educational progress, and occupations;

2. Appraisal activities which means selecting, administering, scoring, and interpreting instruments designed to assess a person's aptitudes, attitudes, abilities, achievements, interests, and personal characteristics, except that nothing in this subdivision authorizes a certified professional counselor to engage in the practice of clinical psychology as defined in Neb. Rev. Stat. §71-1,222;

3. Referral activities which evaluate data to identify which persons or groups may better be served by other specialists;

4. Research activities which means reporting, designing, conducting, or consulting on research in counseling with human subjects;

5. Therapeutic, vocational, or personal rehabilitation in relationship to adapting to physical, emotional, or intellectual disability; and 6. Consulting on any activity listed in this section.

Nevada

Nevada State Board of Massage Therapists
1755 E. Plumb Lane Suite 252
Reno, NV 89502
(775) 687-9955
Fax (775) 786-4264
nvmassagebd@state.nv.us
www.massagetherapy.nv.gov

NRS 640C.020   *Definitions.*
NRS 640C.060   *"Massage therapy" defined.*
1. *"Massage therapy" means the application of a system of pressure to the muscular structure and soft tissues of the human body for therapeutic purposes, including, without limitation:*
   (a) Effleurage;
   (b) Petrissage;
   (c) Tapotement;
   (d) Compressions;
   (e) Vibration;
   (f) Friction; and
   (g) Movements applied manually with or without superficial heat, cold, water or lubricants for the purpose of maintaining good health and establishing and maintaining good physical condition.
   2. The term does not include:
   (a) Diagnosis, adjustment, mobilization or manipulation of any articulations of the body or spine; or
   (b) Reflexology.

Board of Examiners for Marriage & Family Therapists and Clinical Professional Counselors
3436 West Lake Mead Blvd, #11-J
Las Vegas NV 89134-8342

Laws Governing Energy Medicine Practitioners

(702) 486-7388
nvmftbd@mftbd.nev.gov
http://marriage.nv.gov/Board

NRS 641A.065 "Practice of clinical professional counseling" defined.
  1. "Practice of clinical professional counseling" means the provision of treatment, assessment and counseling, or equivalent activities, to a person or group of persons to achieve mental, emotional, physical and social development and adjustment.
  2. The term includes:
  (a) Counseling interventions to prevent, diagnose and treat mental, emotional or behavioral disorders and associated distresses which interfere with mental health; and
  (b) The assessment or treatment of couples or families, if the assessment or treatment is provided by a person who, through the completion of coursework or supervised training or experience, has demonstrated competency in the assessment or treatment of couples or families as determined by the Board.
  3. The term does not include:
  (a) The practice of psychology or medicine;
  (b) The prescription of drugs or electroconvulsive therapy;
  (c) The treatment of physical disease, injury or deformity;
  (d) The diagnosis or treatment of a psychotic disorder;
  (e) The use of projective techniques in the assessment of personality;
  (f) The use of psychological, neuropsychological or clinical tests designed to identify or classify abnormal or pathological human behavior;
  (g) The use of individually administered intelligence tests, academic achievement tests or neuropsychological tests; or
  (h) The use of psychotherapy to treat the concomitants of organic illness except in consultation with a qualified physician or licensed clinical psychologist.
  (Added to NRS by *2007, 3052*; A *2013, 540*)

New Hampshire

New Hampshire Department of Health and Human Services
129 Pleasant Street
Concord, NH 03301-3852
http://www.dhhs.nh.gov/

TITLE XXX
OCCUPATIONS AND PROFESSIONS
CHAPTER 328-B
MASSAGE THERAPISTS AND MASSAGE ESTABLISHMENTS
Section 328-B:2
328-B:2 Definitions
VI. "Massage" means the application of a system of structured touch which includes holding, pressure, positioning, or causing movement, by manual means, for the purpose of promoting, maintaining, and restoring the health and well-being of the client. Massage is designed to promote general relaxation, improve movement, relieve somatic and muscular pain or dysfunction, stress and muscle tension, and provide for general health enhancement, personal growth, and the organization, balance, and integration of the body.

328-B:10 Exemptions; Application of Chapter. –
I. Nothing in this chapter shall prevent a person licensed by this state pursuant to any other provision of law, or any person employed by such a licensee as an assistant, from performing the occupation for which he or she is licensed.
II. Nothing in this chapter shall be construed to prevent or restrict the practice of any person in this state who uses touch, words, and directed movement to deepen awareness of existing patterns of movement as well as to suggest new possibilities of movement, while engaged within the scope of practice of a profession with established standards and ethics, provided that their services are not designated as or implied to be massage or massage therapy. Such practices include, but are not limited to the Feldenkrais method of somatic education, the Trager approach to movement education, the Alexander technique, and body-mind centering.

III. Nothing in this chapter shall be construed to prevent or restrict the practice of any person in this state who uses energy or superficial touch to affect the energy systems of the human body while engaged within the scope of practice of a profession with established standards and ethics, provided that their services are not designated as or implied to be massage or massage therapy. Such practices include, but are not limited to, polarity therapy, therapeutic touch, and reiki.

New Hampshire Board of Mental Health Practice
121 South Fruit Street
Concord, NH 03301
603-271-6762
bdmhp@nh.gov
www.nh.gov/mhpb/

CHAPTER 330-A: MENTAL HEALTH PRACTICE
330-A:2 Definitions. – In this chapter:
I. "Alternative provider" means a person who, for remuneration, engages in any aspect of mental health practice as defined in RSA 330-A:2, VI, but does not hold a license issued under this chapter to practice as a licensed pastoral psychotherapist, clinical social worker, clinical mental health counselor, or marriage and family therapist, and who has registered with the board prior to July 1, 2007.
VI. "Mental health practice" means the observation, description, evaluation, interpretation, diagnosis, and modification of human behavior by the application of psychological and systems principles, methods, and procedures for the purpose of preventing or eliminating symptomatic, maladapted, or undesirable behavior and of enhancing interpersonal relationships, work and life adjustments, personal effectiveness, behavioral health, and mental health, as well as the diagnosis and treatment of the psychological and social aspects of physical illness, accident, injury, or disability. Mental health practice may include, but shall not be limited to, those services based on diagnosis and treatment of mental and emotional disorders and psycho-educational or consultative techniques integral to the treatment of such disorders when diagnosis is specified in the most current edition of the Diagnostic and Statistical Manual of Mental Disorders, published by the American Psychiatric

Association, or an equivalent of such manual as determined by the board. Notwithstanding any other provision to the contrary, no person licensed or registered under this chapter shall assess the need for medications, prescribe medications, or otherwise practice medicine as defined in RSA 329.

VIII. "Psychotherapist" means a clinical social worker, pastoral psychotherapist, clinical mental health counselor, or marriage and family therapist licensed under this chapter who performs or purports to perform psychotherapy. This definition shall include psychiatrists licensed as physicians under RSA 329 and advanced registered nurse practitioners licensed under RSA 326-B:18 as psychiatric nurse practitioners.

IX. "Psychotherapy" means the professional treatment, assessment, or counseling of a mental or emotional illness, symptom, or condition.

New Jersey

New Jersey Board of Massage and Bodywork Therapy
PO Box 47032
Newark, NJ 07101
(973) 504-6520
http://www.state.nj.us/oag/ca/mbt/

45:11-55 Definitions relative to massage, bodywork, somatic therapists [Effective until adoption of rules]. As used in this act:
"Massage, bodywork and somatic therapies" or "massage, bodywork and somatic" means systems of activity of structured touch which include, but are not limited to, holding, applying pressure, positioning and mobilizing soft tissue of the body by manual technique and use of visual, kinesthetic, auditory and palpating skills to assess the body for purposes of applying therapeutic massage, bodywork or somatic principles. Such application may include, but is not limited to, the use of therapies such as heliotherapy or hydrotherapy, the use of moist hot and cold external applications, external application of herbal or topical preparations not classified as prescription drugs, explaining and describing myofascial movement, self-care and stress management as it relates to massage, bodywork and somatic therapies. Massage, bodywork and somatic therapy practices are designed to affect the energetic system of the body for the purpose of promoting and maintaining the health and well-being of the client. Massage, bodywork and somatic therapies do not include the diagnosis or treatment of illness, disease, impairment or disability.

New Jersey Board of Professional Counselors
Board of Marriage and Family Therapy Examiners
Professional Counselor Examiners Committee
P.O. Box 45007
Newark, NJ 07101
973/504-6582
973/648-3536 (fax)
www.njconsumeraffairs.gov/proc
www.state.nj.us/lps/ca/laws/profcounlaws.pdf

45:8B-36. Definitions relative to counseling

4. As used in this act:

"Counseling" means offering to assist or assisting, for a fee or other compensation, an individual or group through a counseling relationship to develop an understanding of interpersonal and intra personal problems and to plan and act on a course of action to restore optimal functioning to that individual or group but does not mean rehabilitation counseling.

45:8B-48. Construction of act

15. Nothing in this act shall be construed to apply to:

a. The activities and services of qualified members of other professions, including physicians, psychologists, registered nurses, marriage and family therapists, attorneys, social workers or any other professionals licensed by the State, when acting within the scope of their profession and doing work of a nature consistent with their training, provided they do not hold themselves out to the public as possessing a license issued pursuant to this act or represent themselves by any professional title regulated by this act.

e. The activities and services of a rabbi, priest, minister, Christian Science practitioner or clergyman of any religious denomination or sect, if those activities and services are within the scope of the performance of his regular or specialized ministerial duties and for which no separate charge is made, or when these activities are performed with or without charge, for or under auspices or sponsorship, individually or in conjunction with others, of an established and legally cognizable church, denomination, or sect, and when the person rendering the service remains accountable to the established authority thereof.

New Mexico

NMCAAMP LLC
P.O. Box 23446
Albuquerque, NM 87192
info@nmcaamp.org
http://www.nmcaamp.org/

RELATING TO HEALTH CARE; ENACTING THE UNLICENSED HEALTH CARE PRACTICE ACT; PROVIDING PENALTIES. BE IT ENACTED BY THE LEGISLATURE OF THE STATE OF NEW MEXICO:
Section 1. SHORT TITLE.--This act may be cited as the "Unlicensed Health Care Practice Act".
Section 2. DEFINITIONS.--As used in the Unlicensed Health Care Practice Act:
A. "complementary and alternative health care practitioner" means an individual who provides complementary and alternative health care services;
B. "complementary and alternative health care service" means the broad domain of complementary and alternative healing methods and treatments including:
(1) anthroposophy;
(2) aromatherapy;
(3) ayurveda;
(4) culturally traditional healing practices, including practices by a curandera, sobadora, partera, medica and arbolaira, and healing traditions, including plant medicines and foods, prayer, ceremony and song; (5) detoxification practices and therapies;
(6) energetic healing; HHGAC/HB 664 Page 2
(7) folk practices;
(8) Gerson therapy and colostrum therapy;
(9) healing practices utilizing food, dietary supplements, nutrients and the physical forces of heat, cold, water, touch and light;
(10) healing touch;
(11) herbology or herbalism;
(12) homeopathy;

(13) meditation;
(14) mind-body healing practices;
(15) naturopathy;
(16) nondiagnostic iridology;
(17) noninvasive instrumentalities;
(18) polarity therapy; and
(19) holistic kinesiology and other muscle testing techniques;
G. "health care practitioner" means an individual who provides health care services;
H. "health care service" means any service relating to the physical and mental health and wellness of an individual;
Section 4. PROHIBITED ACTS.--A complementary and alternative health care practitioner shall not:
A. perform surgery on an individual;
B. set fractures on an individual;
C. administer x-ray radiation to an individual;
D. prescribe or dispense dangerous drugs or controlled substances to an individual;
E. directly manipulate the joints or spine of an individual
F. physically invade the body except for the use of non-prescription topical creams, oils, salves, ointments, tinctures or any other preparations that may penetrate the skin without causing harm;
G. make a recommendation to discontinue current medical treatment prescribed by a licensed health care practitioner
; H. make a specific conventional medical diagnosis; HHGAC/HB 664 Page 5
I. have sexual contact with a current patient or former patient within one year of rendering service;
J. falsely advertise or provide false information in documents described in Subsection A of Section 5 of the Unlicensed Health Care Practice Act;
K. illegally use dangerous drugs or controlled substances;
L. reveal confidential information of a patient without the patient's written consent;
M. engage in fee splitting or kickbacks for referrals;
N. refer to the practitioner's self as a licensed doctor or physician or other occupational title pursuant to Chapter 61 NMSA 1978; or

Laws Governing Energy Medicine Practitioners

O. perform massage therapy on an individual pursuant to the Massage Therapy Practice Act.

Section 5. COMPLEMENTARY AND ALTERNATIVE HEALTH CARE PRACTITIONER--DUTIES.--Except for persons providing health care services pursuant to Section 61-6-17 NMSA 1978 or to employees or persons acting pursuant to the direction of licensed health care facilities or licensed health care providers while working within the scope of their employment or direction, a complementary and alternative health care practitioner shall:

A. provide to a patient prior to rendering HHGAC/HB 664 Page 6 services a patient information document, either in writing in plain language that the patient understands or, if the patient cannot read, orally in a language the patient understands, containing the following:

(1) the complementary and alternative health care practitioner's name, title and business address and telephone number;

(2) a statement that the complementary and alternative health care practitioner is not a health care practitioner licensed by the state of New Mexico;

(3) a statement that the treatment to be provided by the complementary and alternative health care practitioner is complementary or alternative to health care services provided by health care practitioners licensed by the state of New Mexico;

(4) the nature and expected results of the complementary and alternative health care services to be provided;

(5) the complementary and alternative health care practitioner's degrees, education, training, experience or other qualifications regarding the complementary and alternative health care services to be provided;

(6) the complementary and alternative health care practitioner's fees per unit of service and method of billing for such fees and a statement that the patient has a HHGAC/HB 664 Page 7 right to reasonable notice of changes in complementary and alternative health care services or charges for complementary and alternative health care services;

(7) a notice that the patient has a right to complete and current information concerning the complementary and alternative health care practitioner's assessment and recommended complementary and alternative health care services that are to be provided, including the expected duration of the complementary and alternative

health care services to be provided and the patient's right to be allowed access to the patient's records and written information from the patient's records; (8) a statement that patient records and transactions with the complementary and alternative health care practitioner are confidential unless the release of these records is authorized in writing by the patient or otherwise provided by law;

(9) a statement that the patient has a right to coordinated transfer when there will be a change in the provider of complementary and alternative health care services; and

(10) the name, address and telephone number of the department and notice that a patient may file complaints with the department; and B. obtain a written acknowledgment from a patient, HHGAC/HB 664 Page 8 or if the patient cannot write an oral acknowledgment witnessed by a third party, stating that the patient has been provided with a copy of the information document. The patient shall be provided with a copy of the written acknowledgment, which shall be maintained for three years by the complementary and alternative health care practitioner providing the complementary and alternative health care service.

Section 6. APPLICABILITY.--The following individuals shall not provide complementary and alternative health care services pursuant to the Unlicensed Health Care Practice Act:

A. former health care practitioners whose license, certification or registration has been revoked or suspended by any health care board and not reinstated;

B. individuals convicted of a felony for a crime against a person who have not satisfied the terms of the person's sentence as provided by law;

C. individuals convicted of a felony related to health care who have not satisfied the terms of the person's sentence as provided by law; and

D. individuals who have been deemed mentally incompetent by a court of law.

Section 7. DISCIPLINARY ACTIONS.--If the department determines that a complementary and alternative health care practitioner practicing pursuant to the Unlicensed Health Care Practice Act may have violated a provision of that act, it may HHGAC/HB 664 Page 9 take one or more of the following actions pursuant to the Uniform Licensing Act against the complementary and alternative health care practitioner if that practitioner is found to have violated a provision of the Unlicensed Health Care Practice Act:

Laws Governing Energy Medicine Practitioners

A. provide written notice to the complementary and alternative health care practitioner requesting the practitioner to correct the activity that is a violation of the Unlicensed Health Care Practice Act; this action shall be the first option if the offense is a violation of the disclosure requirements of the Unlicensed Health Care Practice Act;

B. issue a cease and desist order against the complementary and alternative health care practitioner pertaining to the provision of complementary and alternative health care services that are not in compliance with the provisions of the Unlicensed Health Care Practitioner Act; or

C. impose a civil penalty in an amount not to exceed ten thousand dollars ($10,000) for each violation. Section 8. DUTIES OF THE SUPERINTENDENT.--The superintendent of regulation and licensing is expressly authorized to promulgate rules as necessary to implement the provisions of the Unlicensed Health Care Practice Act. Section 9. SEVERABILITY.--If any part or application of this act is held invalid, the remainder or its application to other situations or persons shall not be affected. Section 10. EFFECTIVE DATE.--The effective date of the provisions of this act is July 1, 2009.

New York

NY State Education Department
Office of the Professions
Division of Professional Licensing Services
Massage Therapy Unit
89 Washington Avenue
Albany, New York 12234-1000
518-474-3817, ext. 270 (voice)
518-402-5354 (fax)
opunit3@nysed.gov

7801. Definition of practice of massage therapy.

The practice of the profession of massage therapy is defined as engaging in applying a scientific system of activity to the muscular structure of the human body by means of stroking, kneading, tapping and vibrating with the hands or vibrators for the purpose of improving muscle tone and circulation.

I found no mention of exemptions for energy healers.

NY State Education Department
Office of the Professions
Division of Professional Licensing Services
Mental Health Practitioners Unit
89 Washington Avenue
Albany, New York 12234-1000
518-474-3817 ext. 592 (voice)
518-402-2323 (fax)
opunit5@nysed.gov

8401. Definitions
"Psychotherapy" means the treatment of mental, nervous, emotional, behavioral and addictive disorders, and ailments by the use of both verbal and behavioral

methods of intervention in interpersonal relationships with the intent of assisting the persons to modify attitudes, thinking, affect, and behavior which are intellectually, socially and emotionally maladaptive.

8402. Mental health counseling.
1. *Definition of the practice of mental health counseling. The practice of the profession of mental health counseling is defined as:*
a. *the evaluation, assessment, amelioration, treatment, modification, or adjustment to a disability, problem, or disorder of behavior, character, development, emotion, personality or relationships by the use of verbal or behavioral methods with individuals, couples, families or groups in private practice, group, or organized settings; and*
b. *the use of assessment instruments and mental health counseling and psychotherapy to identify, evaluate and treat dysfunctions and disorders for purposes of providing appropriate mental health counseling services.*
2. *Practice of mental health counseling and use of the titles "mental health counselor" and "licensed mental health counselor". Only a person licensed or exempt under this article shall practice mental health counseling or use the title "mental health counselor". Only a person licensed under this article shall use the title "licensed mental health counselor" or any other designation tending to imply that the person is licensed to practice mental health counseling.*

8410. Exemptions.
Nothing contained in this article shall be construed to:
1. *Apply to the practice, conduct, activities, services or use of any title by any person licensed or otherwise authorized to practice medicine within the state pursuant to article one hundred thirty-one of this title or by any person registered to perform services as a physician assistant within the state pursuant to article one hundred thirty-one-B of this title or by any person licensed or otherwise authorized to practice psychology within this state pursuant to article one hundred fifty-three of this title or by any person licensed or otherwise authorized to practice social work within this state pursuant to article one hundred fifty-four of this title, or by any person licensed or otherwise authorized to practice*

nursing as a registered professional nurse or nurse practitioner within this state pursuant to article one hundred thirty-nine of this title or by any person licensed or otherwise authorized to practice applied behavior analysis within the state pursuant to article one hundred sixty-seven of this title; provided, however, that no physician, physician's assistant, registered professional nurse, nurse practitioner, psychologist, licensed master social worker, licensed clinical social worker, licensed behavior analyst or certified behavior analyst assistant may use the titles "licensed mental health counselor", "licensed marriage and family therapist", "licensed creative arts therapist", or "licensed psychoanalyst", unless licensed under this article.

2. *Prohibit or limit the provision of pastoral counseling services by any member of the clergy or Christian Science practitioner, within the context of his or her ministerial charge or obligation.*

3. *Prevent a person without a license from performing assessments such as basic information collection, gathering of demographic data, and informal observations, screening and referral used for general eligibility for a program or service and determining the functional status of an individual for the purpose of determining need for services unrelated to a behavioral health diagnosis or treatment plan. Such licensure shall not be required to create, develop or implement a service plan unrelated to a behavioral health diagnosis or treatment plan. Such service plans shall include, but are not limited to, job training and employability, housing, general public assistance, in home services and supports or home-delivered meals, investigations conducted or assessments made by adult or child protective services, adoption home studies and assessments, family service plans, transition plans and permanency planning activities, de-escalation techniques, peer services or skill development. A license under this article shall not be required for persons to participate as a member of a multi-disciplinary team to implement a behavioral health services or treatment plan; provided however, that such team shall include one or more professionals licensed under this article or articles one hundred thirty-one, one hundred fifty-three or one hundred fifty-four of this chapter; and provided, further, that the activities performed by members of the team shall be consistent with the scope of practice for each team member licensed or authorized under title VIII of this chapter,*

and those who are not so authorized may not engage in the following restricted practices: the diagnosis of mental, emotional, behavioral, addictive and developmental disorders and disabilities; patient assessment and evaluating; the provision of psychotherapeutic treatment; the provision of treatment other than psychotherapeutic treatment; and/or the development and implementation of assessment-based treatment plans as defined in section seventy-seven hundred one of this chapter. Provided, further, that nothing in this subdivision shall be construed as requiring a license for any particular activity or function based solely on the fact that the activity or function is not listed in this subdivision.

North Carolina

North Carolina Board of Massage & Bodywork Therapy
Address: 150 Fayetteville
St, Raleigh, NC 27601
Phone:(919) 546-0050
www.bmbt.org

ARTICLE 36 Massage and Bodywork Therapy Practice
90-622. Definitions. The following definitions apply in this Article:
Massage and bodywork therapy. Systems of activity applied to the soft tissues of the human body for therapeutic, educational, or relaxation purposes. The application may include: a. Pressure, friction, stroking, rocking, kneading, percussion, or passive or active stretching within the normal anatomical range of movement. b Complementary methods, including the external application of water, heat, cold, lubricants, and other topical preparations. c. The use of mechanical devices that mimic or enhance actions that may possibly be done by the hands.
90-624. Exemptions.
7. The practice of techniques that are specifically intended to affect human energy field.

.0203 EXEMPTIONS FROM LICENSURE (a) Persons who are utilizing certain therapeutic techniques may claim exemption from licensure pursuant to G.S. 90-624 (6) or (7) only by meeting one of the following criteria: (1) Such persons are practicing techniques that are defined by national organizations that meet the criteria for exemption set forth in either G.S. 90-624 (6) or (7); or (2) Such persons are practicing techniques that do not involve any contact with the body of the client; or (3) Such persons are practicing techniques that involve resting the hands on the surface of the client's body without delivering pressure to or manipulation of the soft tissues.

North Carolina Board of Licensed Professional Counselors
PO Box 77819
Greensboro NC 27417
(844) 622-3572
http://www.ncblpc.org/

Article 24. Licensed Professional Counselors Act.
90-330. Definitions; practice of counseling.
The "practice of counseling" means holding oneself out to the public as a professional counselor offering counseling services that include, but are not limited to, the following: a. Counseling. – Assisting individuals, groups, and families through the counseling relationship by evaluating and treating mental disorders and other conditions through the use of a combination of clinical mental health and human development principles, methods, diagnostic procedures, treatment plans, and other psychotherapeutic techniques, to develop an understanding of personal problems, to define goals, and to plan action reflecting the client's interests, abilities, aptitudes, and mental health needs as these are related to personal-social-emotional concerns, educational progress, and occupations and careers. b. Appraisal Activities. – Administering and interpreting tests for assessment of personal characteristics. c. Consulting. – Interpreting scientific data and providing guidance and personnel services to individuals, groups, or organizations. d. Referral Activities. – Identifying problems requiring referral to other specialists. e. Research Activities. – Designing, conducting, and interpreting research with human subjects.

90-332.1. Exemptions from licensure.
Any ordained minister or other member of the clergy while acting in a ministerial capacity who does not charge a fee for the service, or any person invited by a religious organization to conduct, lead, or provide counseling to its members when the service is not performed for more than 30 days a year.

North Dakota

North Dakota State Board of Massage
PO Box 218
Beach, ND 58621
phone: 1-877-268-8139
email: karen.wojahn@ndboardofmassage.com
www.ndboardofmassage.com/

CHAPTER 43-25 MASSAGE THERAPISTS
43-25-02. *Definitions*
"*Massage*" *means the scientific and systematic manipulation of the soft tissues of the human body through any manual or mechanical means, using western and eastern modalities, including superficial hot and cold applications, hydrotherapy, reflexology, shiatsu, acupressure, and the use of salts or lubricants for the purpose of promoting, maintaining, and restoring the health and well-being of the client. The term includes assessment, effleurage (stroking or gliding), petrissage (kneading), tapotement (percussion), compression, vibration, friction, and active or passive range of motion and stretching either by hand, forearm, elbow, knee, foot, or with mechanical appliances for the purpose of body massage. Except as provided in this chapter, "massage" does not include diagnosis or other services that require a license to practice medicine or surgery, osteopathic medicine, chiropractic, occupational therapy, physical therapy, or podiatry and does not include service provided by professionals who act under their state-issued professional license, certification, or registration. 3. "Massage establishment" means any place of business in which massage is practice*
43-25-04. *Exemptions. The following persons are exempt from this chapter:*
Any individual practicing healing by manipulating the energy field or the flow of energy of the human body by means other than the manipulation of the soft tissues of the human body, provided that the individual's services are not designated or implied to be massage or massage therapy. For purposes of this subsection, a light touch or tap is not a manipulation of the soft tissues of the human body.

North Dakota Board - Counselors

2112 10th Ave SE
Mandan, ND 58554
(701) 667-5969
http://www.ndbce.org/

CHAPTER 43-47 COUNSELORS
43-47-01. Definitions. As used in this chapter, unless the context otherwise requires: "Counseling" means the application of human development and mental health principles in a therapeutic process and professional relationship to assist individuals, couples, families, and groups in achieving more effective emotional, mental, marital, family, and social or educational development and adjustment. The goals of professional counseling are to: a. Facilitate human development and adjustment throughout the lifespan; b. Prevent, assess, and treat emotional, mental, or behavioral disorder and distress which interferes with mental health; c. Conduct assessments for the purpose of establishing treatment goals and objectives; and d. Plan, implement, and evaluate treatment plans using professional counseling strategies and interventions.
43-47-05. Counseling practice - Exceptions.
This chapter does not prevent any person licensed by the state from doing work within the standards and ethics of that person's profession, if that person does not represent to the public that the person is a professional counselor or associate professional counselor
This chapter does not prevent a member of the clergy of any religious denomination from providing services within the scope of ministerial duties.

Ohio

Ohio Medical Board of Massage Therapy
30 East Broad St. 3rd Floor
Columbus, OH 43215
Phone: 614-466-3934
http://codes.ohio.gov/

Ohio is the only state in which massage therapy is considered a limited branch of medicine.

Chapter 4731-1 Limited Branches of Medicine or Surgery
4731-1-01 Definition of terms.

(A) Massage therapy is the treatment of disorders of the human body by the manipulation of soft tissue through the systematic external application of massage techniques including touch, stroking, friction, vibration, percussion, kneading, stretching, compression, and joint movements within the normal physiologic range of motion; and adjunctive thereto, the external application of water, heat, cold, topical preparations, and mechanical devices.

(B) A massage therapist shall not diagnose a patient's condition. A massage therapist shall evaluate whether the application of massage therapy is advisable. A massage therapist may provide information or education consistent with that evaluation, including referral to an appropriate licensed health care professional, provided that any form of treatment advised by a massage therapist falls within the scope of practice of, and relates directly to a condition that is amenable to treatment by, a massage therapist. In determining whether the application of massage therapy is advisable, a massage therapist shall be limited to taking a written or verbal inquiry, visual inspection including observation of range of motion, touch, and the taking of a pulse, temperature and blood pressure.

Counselor Social Worker & Marriage and Family Therapist Board
50 West Broad Street, Suite 1075
Columbus, Ohio 43215-3344
(614) 466-0912
cswmft.info@cswb.ohio.gov
http://cswmft.ohio.gov/

Ohio Revised Code Chapter 4757: COUNSELORS, SOCIAL WORKERS, MARRIAGE AND FAMILY THERAPISTS 4757.01 Counselor, social worker, and marriage and family therapist definitions. As used in this chapter:
"Practice of professional counseling" means rendering or offering to render to individuals, groups, organizations, or the general public a counseling service involving the application of clinical counseling principles, methods, or procedures to assist individuals in achieving more effective personal, social, educational, or career development and adjustment, including the diagnosis and treatment of mental and emotional disorders.
4757.41 Exemptions.
(3) Members of other professions licensed, certified, or registered by this state while performing services within the recognized scope, standards, and ethics of their respective professions; (4) Rabbis, priests, Christian science practitioners, clergy, or members of religious orders and other individuals participating with them in pastoral counseling when the counseling activities are within the scope of the performance of their regular or specialized ministerial duties and are performed under the auspices or sponsorship of an established and legally cognizable church, denomination, or sect or an integrated auxiliary of a church as defined in federal tax regulations, paragraph (g)(5) of 26 C.F.R. 1.6033-2 (1995), and when the individual rendering the service remains accountable to the established authority of that church, denomination, sect, or integrated auxiliary;

Oklahoma

Oklahoma has no statewide regulations for massage parlors, but Oklahoma City, Tulsa, Moore, Lawton and Stillwater do have ordinances designed to stop illegal sex acts and ensure safe massages for customers.
Oklahoma City is the only municipality in the Oklahoma City-County Department's (OCCHD) jurisdiction that requires a license for massage establishments and for individuals to perform massage within Oklahoma City city limits.

State Board of Behavioral Health
3815 N. Santa Fe, Suite 110
Oklahoma City, OK 73118.
(405) 522- 3696
www.ok.gov/behavioralhealth

Section 1902. Definitions For the purpose of the Licensed Professional Counselors Act: "Counseling" means the application of mental health and developmental principles in order to: a. Facilitate human development and adjustment throughout the life span, b. prevent, diagnose or treat mental, emotional or behavioral disorders or associated distress which interfere with mental health, c. conduct assessments or diagnoses for the purpose of establishing treatment goals and objectives, and d. plan, implement or evaluate treatment plans using counseling treatment interventions; "Counseling treatment interventions" means the application of cognitive, affective, behavioral and systemic counseling strategies which include principles of development, wellness, and pathology that reflect a pluralistic society. Such interventions are specifically implemented in the context of a professional counseling relationship;

Oregon

Oregon Board of Massage Therapists
748 Hawthorne Avenue NE
Salem OR 97301
(503) 365-8657
OBMT.Info@state.or.us

687.011 Definitions. As used in ORS 687.011 to 687.250, 687.895 and 687.991:
(3) "Manual" means the use of the hands, feet or any other part of the body in the performance of massage.
(4) "Massage" or "massage therapy" means the use of pressure, friction, stroking, tapping or kneading on the human body, or the use of vibration or stretching on the human body by manual or mechanical means or gymnastics, with or without appliances such as vibrators, infrared heat, sun lamps or external baths, and with or without lubricants such as salts, powders, liquids or creams, for the purpose of, but not limited to, maintaining good health and establishing and maintaining good physical condition.

687.031 Application of ORS 687.011 to 687.250, 687.895 and 687.991. (1) ORS 687.011 to 687.250, 687.895 and 687.991 **do not apply to***:*
(h) Trained or licensed practitioners of psychotherapy or counseling modalities that use physical techniques to access or support psychotherapeutic processes when practicing within the scope of a license or if the practitioner has an express oral or written agreement that the sole intent in using the physical techniques is to render the psychotherapy or counseling.
(i) Practitioners of reflexology who do not claim expressly or implicitly to be massage therapists and who limit their work to the practice of reflexology through the application of pressure with the thumbs to reflex points on the feet, hands and ears for the purpose of bringing the body into balance, thereby promoting the well-being of clients.
(j) Practitioners who:
(A) Do not claim expressly or implicitly to be massage therapists;

(B) Limit their work to one or more of the following practices:
(i) Using touch, words and directed movement to deepen awareness of existing patterns of movement and suggest new possibilities of movement;
(ii) Using minimal touch over specific points on the body to facilitate balance in the nervous system; or
(iii) Using touch to affect the energy systems or channels of energy of the body;
(C) Are certified by a professional organization or credentialing agency that:
(i) Requires a minimum level of training, demonstration of competence and adherence to an approved scope of practice and ethical standards; and
(ii) Maintains disciplinary procedures to ensure adherence to the requirements of the organization or agency; and
(D) Provide contact information in the practitioner's place of business for any organization or agency that has certified the practitioner.

Oregon Board of Licensed Professional Counselors and Therapists
3218 Pringle Road SE, Suite 250
Salem OR 97302-6312
(503) 378-5499
lpct.board@state.or.us
www.oregon.gov?oblpct

I couldn't find a definition of counselor or counseling in the statutes.

Oregon State Board of Nursing
17938 SW Upper Boones Ferry Road
Portland OR 97224-7012
971-673-0685
www.oregon.gov/OSBN

Under nursing I found the following:
Oregon State Board of Nursing
• Board Policy Complementary and Alternative Modalities and Nursing Practice Statement of Purpose To establish guidelines and provide clear direction for Oregon

Laws Governing Energy Medicine Practitioners

licensed nurses who want to practice using complementary or alternative modalities. Background Information There are a number of therapeutic modalities that are intended to improve the health and wellbeing of clients. These modalities are those which licensed nurses may employ to increase comfort or relaxation, maintain, improve or restore health and harmony of the body, mind, and/or spirit, improve coping mechanisms, reduce stress, relieve pain and/or increase the client's sense of well being. They are used either in addition to or in place of conventional treatments. Many of these therapeutic modalities are not regulated by the State of Oregon and, while scientific evidence exists regarding some modalities, it is limited to date. The National Center for Complementary and Alternative Medicine (NCCAM) states that complementary modalities are those used together with conventional medicine and alternative therapies those used in place of conventional medicine. NCCAM says that Integrative Care combines complementary and alternative approaches with conventional medicine. In addition, they divide the modalities into four domains, plus establish a category for whole medical systems, which crosses all domains. These domains are:

- *Manipulative and Body-based Practices*
- *Mind-body Medicine*
- *Biologically-based Practices • Energy Medicine*
- *Whole Medical Systems Specific modalities are listed on both the NCCAM website as well as the American Holistic Nurses Association (AHNA) website. The licensed nurse must be able to determine whether or not a particular modality is within his/her scope of practice and whether or not to incorporate it into practice. The licensed nurse is always expected to be familiar with and adhere to nursing scope and standards of practice as found in the Nurse Practice Act. At times, modalities cross the boundaries of other scopes of practice. When that is the case, confusion and potential liability for the practitioner may exist for practicing outside the scope of practice afforded by current licensure or for practicing without licensure by another health licensing entity. This document will assist the licensed nurse in making determinations regarding these issues.*

Scope of Practice Statement The Oregon State Board of Nursing affirms that it is within the scope of practice for the Registered Nurse (RN) and Licensed Practical Nurse (LPN) to provide complementary and alternative modalities for a client provided the following conditions are met. The LPN carries out these activities only under the direction of the RN or other licensed health care provider who has authority to make changes in the plan of care. The RN/LPN must:

1. Function within the scope of practice standards set for his/her licensure category.

2. Perform a nursing assessment (RN may perform comprehensive or focused assessments and LPNs may perform focused assessments), make a nursing diagnostic statement (LPNs may select diagnostic statements from available resources), and develop a nursing plan of care (The LPN may contribute to care plan development and develop focused plans of care). Both RNs and LPNs are responsible for documentation.

3. Support the client to become an informed consumer. (See below) Page 1 of 5 Oregon State Board of Nursing • Board Policy

4. Obtain the client's permission to utilize the specific modality.

5. Have documented knowledge, judgment, skill and competency in the application of the modality.

6. May provide information for non-prescriptive remedies (such as vitamins, minerals, homeopathic, herbal, compound medications, or over-the-counter drugs) as long as the concepts delineated in "Supporting the Client to Become an Informed Consumer," listed below, are followed.

7. Obtain additional licensure /certification when needed (recommended or required for alternative modalities and some complementary modalities).

8. When employing the use of any modality which is regulated by any other State of Oregon health related Agency, Board or Commission, the licensed nurse must adhere to those statutes and rules pertaining to the modality.

The Oregon State Board of Nursing affirms that it is within the scope of practice of the Nurse Practitioner (NP) and Clinical Nurse Specialist (CNS) to provide complementary and alternative modalities for a client provided the following conditions are met: The NP/CNS must:

1. Always function within the scope of practice standards set for his/her licensure category and specialty area of practice.

2. Perform an assessment consistent with an existing or new diagnosis, and document a treatment plan.

3. Support the client to become an informed consumer. (See below)

4. Obtain the client's permission to utilize the specific modality.

Laws Governing Energy Medicine Practitioners

5. Have documented knowledge, judgment, skill and competency in the application of the modality.

6. If the NP or CNS has prescriptive authority, practice consistent with the Oregon State Board of Nursing Policy entitled, Nurse Practitioners and Clinical Nurse Specialists with Prescriptive Authority and Non-Prescriptive Remedies must be followed.

7. Obtain additional licensure /certification when needed (recommended or required for alternative modalities and some complementary modalities).

8. When employing the use of any modality which is regulated by any other State of Oregon health related Agency, Board or Commission, adhere to those statutes and rules pertaining to the modality.

In addition to the above criteria, when a RN or LPN (under the clinical direction of a RN or other health care professional who has authority to make changes in the plan of care) independently (within that licensed nurse's scope of practice) practices as a provider of a modality, he/she must have written consent. He/she shall also disclose to the client:

1. The nurse's status as a licensed nurse.

2. The educational preparation, experiences and credentials as a therapist/practitioner of the modality.

3. Whether the particular modality is regulated by a state regulatory agency and whether uniform educational standards or requirements have been adopted by that agency.

4. Services are not meant to replace medical care or psychotherapy. When a licensed nurse, functioning within an organized health system, elects to utilize a modality to augment his/her practice, the therapy must be approved by and be consistent with the organization's policies and procedures. The therapy must also be consistent with the mutually established client goals and the overall treatment plan.

Knowledge, Skills and Competency

The licensed nurse must acquire, document and maintain current knowledge, skills and competency in the modalities that will be practiced. The licensed nurse has an accountability to practice complementary or alternative modalities or integrative care in accord with the generally accepted standards of that modality as well as the Page 2 of 5 Oregon State Board of Nursing Board Policy accepted standards of *nursing practice. The nurse must at all times adhere to the statutes and regulations of the particular therapy.*

NPs and CNSs with prescriptive authority for whom the recommendation of non-prescriptive remedies (such as vitamins, minerals, homeopathic, herbal, compound medications, or over-thecounter drugs) constitutes a significant proportion of therapeutic practice should dedicate continuing education hours to reflect these practices. These hours may constitute part of the overall continuing education hours required for NPs and CNSs, but are in addition to the hours required in pharmacology for prescriptive medications.

Supporting the Client to Become an Informed Consumer The client is the primary health care decision maker and may choose to whom, under what circumstances, and for what purpose he/she seeks health care. A licensed nurse, while providing care to a client, may be asked by the client, or discover inadvertently, that the client is either seeking to utilize, or currently utilizing, over-the-counter products or alternative/complementary therapies to supplement or to replace prescriptive medications, treatments and/or therapies. In this instance, the licensed nurse would encourage the client to inform their primary health care provider of the client's actions or intended actions, and encourage the client to acquire accurate information about the over-the-counter products such as:

1. Possible consequences of discontinuing the prescription medication(s).
2. Description and components of the therapy.
3. Safety factors/issues related to the therapy.
4. Potential goals/benefits of the therapy.
5. The potential for the therapy to interact in a non-therapeutic way with the treatment regime established by the primary health care provider.
6. Expected frequency of therapy over what course of time.
7. Expected course of therapy and its total cost.
8. Third party reimbursement. The licensed nurse would educate the consumer that the health care decision-making begins with the client obtaining a complete medical evaluation including current health practices in order to:

Develop a therapeutic treatment plan which enhances the client's health promotion and maintenance; reduces opportunity for untoward side effects or contraindications; and safeguard the client's health.

Laws Governing Energy Medicine Practitioners

Definitions
1. *"Alternative Modalities." A diverse group of therapies and practices used in place of conventional medicine for the purpose of increasing comfort or relaxation, maintaining, improving or restoring health and harmony of the body, mind, and/or spirit, improving coping mechanisms, reducing stress, relieving pain and/or increasing the client's sense of well being.*
2. *"Client." A person who is a consumer of health care services.*
3. *"Complementary Modalities." A diverse group of therapies and practices used together with conventional medicine for the purpose of increasing comfort or relaxation, maintaining, improving or restoring health and harmony of the body, mind, and/or spirit, improving coping mechanisms, reducing stress, relieving pain and/or increasing the client's sense of well being.*
4. *"Integrative Care." The combination of both complementary modalities and alternative approaches with conventional medicine. Integrative care includes multiple modalities in the overall patient-centered plan of care.*
5. *"Licensed Independent Practitioner." An individual permitted by Oregon law to independently make a medical diagnosis, provide care, treatment and services that are within the individual's scope of practice. Page 3 of 5 Oregon State Board of Nursing • Board Policy*
6. *"Licensed Nurse." All RNs and LPNs licensed under ORS 678. In this document, licensed nurse may also apply to the NP and CNS.*
7. *"Nursing Diagnostic Statements. The nursing diagnoses or reasoned conclusions which are developed as a result of nursing assessment. They describe a client's actual or potential health problems which are amendable to resolution by means of nursing strategies, interventions or actions.*

Questions and Answers
1. *Q: Which modalities require separate licensure by the State of Oregon? A: Acupuncture, Massage Therapy, Chiropractic Medicine, Osteopathic Medicine, Naturopathic Medicine, Physical Therapy are all regulated by other health care licensing Boards in Oregon. In addition, there may be other modalities which contain elements that fall within the domain of health care licensing Boards. For example, if a modality included psychotherapy, it would not fall within the scope of the RN or LPN and it would only be appropriate if it fell within the specialty area*

of practice of the NP or CNS. Otherwise, a licensed nurse would have to have dual licensure in another health field, such as clinical social work or psychology, which would enable the nurse to conduct psychotherapy.

2. Q: At times, there is overlap between licensed nursing practice and massage. How does a licensed nurse figure out when he/she needs a separate massage license? A: The Oregon Board of Massage Therapists requires licensure for massage therapy, and limits individual practitioners from using the term "massage" in the business name unless the individual is a Licensed Massage Therapist (LMT). Practically speaking, this means that the licensed nurse should not set up an independent business, advertise for and perform only massage unless also a LMT. However, if massage is conducted as an element of practice within a broader documented nursing plan of care this may be within the licensed nurses' scope of practice.

3. Q: Can a nurse's advertisement for a complementary modality include the word "massage"? A: The word "massage" may not be used in the business name unless the licensed nurse is also a LMT. The licensed nurse may not advertise that he/she performs massage, but may use the word "massage" to describe an element of practice or a technique which would be used in a broader documented nursing plan of care. For example, an appropriate nursing intervention may include massage of an acupressure point. The licensed nurse may choose to refer to "massage" in this limited context in an advertising brochure.

4. Q. Can a licensed nurse independently practice as a provider of complementary or alternative modalities or integrative care? A: This is appropriate for the RN, NP or CNS as long as he/she is working within scope of practice set by licensure category, and given that knowledge, skills and competency are established and documented. The LPN's practice is a directed practice, which means that if he/she were to engage in complementary or alternative modalities or integrative care, that practice would need to be accomplished under the direction of another licensed provider who has authority to make changes in the plan of care.

In addition, the nurse shall also disclose to the client:

1. The nurse's status as a licensed nurse.

2. The educational preparation, experiences and credentials as a therapist/practitioner of the modality.

Laws Governing Energy Medicine Practitioners

3. Whether the particular modality is regulated by a state regulatory agency and whether uniform educational standards or requirements have been adopted by that agency.

4. Services are not meant to replace medical care or psychotherapy. Page 4 of 5 Oregon State Board of Nursing • Board Policy

5. Q: How can I best achieve and be able to demonstrate current knowledge, skills and competency? A: Due to the wide variety of modalities, it is difficult to list one way to achieve and demonstrate competency in a modality. As with other areas of practice, you must understand the theoretical underpinnings of the modality, the practical application/s, possible risks, side effects, etc. and be able to manage the consequences of your actions. Client safety must always be a paramount concern. Some of the modalities require formal education and licensure; others require formal course work and certifying examinations. Other modalities may be presented less formally (e.g. through a conference), but still require an examination. Documentation means that you have to be able to demonstrate on paper how you have achieved the given competency. It does not mean that the practitioner necessarily must be certified, but it does mean that if there were a question about competency, the nurse (all levels of licensure) would be able to demonstrate on paper how he/she had become competent. This could be from coursework or it could be from documented training and mentorship, or a combination.

Important note.
While nurses do have permission to touch while doing energy work in Oregon, their insurance may not cover energy work. Check with your insurance agent.

Pennsylvania

State Board of Massage Therapy
P.O. Box 2649, Harrisburg, PA 17105-2649
Phone - (717) 783-7155
Fax - (717) 787-7769
RA-MASSAGETHERAPY@PA.GOV

MASSAGE THERAPY ACT
ACT 118 OF 2008 (AMENDED BY ACT 45 OF 2009
Section 2. Definitions.
"Healing arts." The science and skill of diagnosis and treatment in any manner whatsoever of disease or any ailment of the human body.
"Massage therapy." The application of a system of structured touch, pressure, movement, holding and treatment of the soft tissue manifestations of the human body in which the primary intent is to enhance the health and well-being of the client without limitation, except as provided in this act. The term includes the external application of water, heat, cold, lubricants or other topical preparations, lymphatic techniques, myofascial release techniques and the use of electro-mechanical devices which mimic or enhance the action of the massage techniques. The term does not include the diagnosis or treatment of impairment, illness, disease or disability, a medical procedure, a chiropractic manipulation - adjustment, physical therapy mobilization - manual therapy, therapeutic exercise, electrical stimulation, ultrasound or prescription of medicines for which a license to practice medicine, chiropractic, physical therapy, occupational therapy, podiatry or other practice of the healing arts is required. "Reflexology." The physical act of using thumbs, fingers and hand techniques to apply specific pressure on the reflex area in the feet, hands or ears of the client.

Section 13. Other professions. Nothing in this act shall be construed as preventing, restricting or requiring licensure of any of the following activities:
(4) The practice by an individual while performing reflexology.

Laws Governing Energy Medicine Practitioners

(5) The practice of an individual who uses touch, words and directed movement to deepen awareness of existing patterns of movement in the body and to suggest new possibilities of movement, while engaged within the scope of practice of a profession with established standards and ethics.

(6) The practice of an individual who uses touch to affect the energy systems, acupoints, Qi meridians or channels of energy of the human body while engaged within the scope of practice of a profession with established standards and ethics. Such practices include acupressure, Asian bodywork therapy, polarity therapy bodywork, quigon, reiki, shiatsu and tui na.

State Board of Social Workers, Marriage and Family Therapists and Professional Counselors
P.O. Box 2649, Harrisburg, PA 17105-2649
Phone - (717) 783-1389
Fax - (717) 787-7769
ST-SOCIALWORK@PA.GOV
I couldn't find any clear cut definitions of counselor or counseling. No exemptions listed in the statutes either..

Puerto Rico

Puerto Rico Board of Examiners of Massage Therapists
Calle Rafael Cordero #154
Oficina Num. 500
Viejo San Juan San Juan PR 00902-3271
(787) 725-8538

Section 2.– Definitions: For purposes of this Act, the following terms and phrases shall have the *meanings stated below:*
"Massage Therapy" – means a system of structured manipulation for therapeutic, preventive and remedial purposes through scientific and skilled manipulation of superficial or deep soft tissue to promote general relaxation, improve circulation, joint mobility, soothe stress and muscular tension and generally promote physical, mental and emotional wellbeing. The term and its practice include manual, mechanical and technical procedures generally accepted in the practice of massage, including but not limited to, rubbing, stroking, rocking, pressure, tapping, kneading, stretching and other techniques developed under the concept of bodywork, which may use the application of oils, salts, compresses and other externally applied products that ease movement. Excluded from this definition are those practices and techniques that are exclusive to the profession of Physical Therapy.
Section 19.– Exceptions Excluded from the requirements of this Act, shall be the practice of massage within osteopathic medicine, physical therapy, naturopathy, or any other branch of medicine in which the practice of massage has been regulated by Law, provided this is within the context of the regular medical treatment, and not as part of a therapeutic massage business.

Puerto Rico Board of Examiners of Professional Counselors
P.O. Box 10200
San Juan, PR 00908
787/765-2929
www.salud.gov.pr

The web site is in Spanish. I couldn't find anything in English.

Rhode Island

State of Rhode Island Department of Health
Board of Massage Therapy
3 Capitol Hill, Room 104
Providence RI 02908-5097
(401) 222-2828
http://www.health.ri.gov/applications/MassageTherapist.pdf

PART I Licensing Requirements for Massage Therapists
Section 1.0 Definitions
"The practice of massage" means engaging in applying a scientific system of activity to the 2 muscular structure of the human body by means of stroking, kneading, tapping and vibrating with the hands or vibrators for the purpose of improving muscle tone and circulation.

Persons Exempt 2.1.1 Nothing contained in the Act shall prohibit:
(1) The practice of massage by any person who is authorized to practice medicine, nursing, osteopathy, physiotherapy, chiropractic, or podiatry in this state.

CHAPTER 23-74
Unlicensed Health Care Practices
SECTION 23-74-1
23-74-1 Definitions and applicability. – *(a) As used in this chapter, the following terms have the following meanings:*
(3) "Unlicensed health care practices" means the broad domain of unlicensed healing methods and treatments, including, but not limited to: (i) acupressure; (ii) Alexander technique; (iii) aroma therapy; (iv) ayurveda; (v) cranial sacral therapy; (vi) crystal therapy; (vii) detoxification practices and therapies; (viii) energetic healing; (ix) rolfing; (x) Gerson therapy and colostrum therapy; (xi) therapeutic touch; (xii) herbology or herbalism; (xiii) polarity therapy; (xiv) homeopathy; (xv) nondiagnostic iridology; (xvi) body work; (xvii) reiki; (xviii) mind-body healing practices; (ixx) naturopathy; and (xx) Qi Gong energy healing. "Unlicensed health

care practices" do not include surgery, x-ray radiation, prescribing, administering, or dispensing legend drugs and controlled substances, practices that invade the human body by puncture of the skin, setting fractures, any practice included in the practice of dentistry, the manipulation or adjustment of articulations of joints, or the spine, also known as chiropractic medicine as defined in chapter 30 of title 5, the healing art of acupuncture as defined in chapter 37.2 of title 5, or practices that are permitted under § 5-37-15 or § 5-34-31(6).

(4) "Unlicensed health care practitioner" means a person who:

(i) Is not licensed by a health-related licensing board or the director of health; or holds a license issued by a health-related licensing board or the department of health in this state, but does not hold oneself out to the public as being licensed or registered by the director or a health-related licensing board when engaging in unlicensed health care;

(ii) Has not had a license issued by a health-related licensing board or the director of health revoked or suspended without reinstatement unless the right to engage in unlicensed health care practices has been established by order of the director of health;

(iii) Is engaging in unlicensed health care practices; and

(iv) Is providing unlicensed health care services for remuneration or is holding oneself out to the public as a practitioner of unlicensed health care practices.

(b) This chapter does not apply to, control, prevent, or restrict the practice, service, or activity of lawfully marketing or distributing food products, including dietary supplements as defined in the federal Dietary Supplement Health and Education Act [see 21 U.S.C. § 321(ff)], educating customers about those products, or explaining the uses of those products. Under Rhode Island law, an unlicensed health care practitioner may not provide a medical diagnosis.

(c) A health care practitioner, licensed or registered by the director or a health-related licensing board, who engages in unlicensed health care while practicing under the practitioner's license or registration, shall be regulated by and be under the jurisdiction of the applicable health-related licensing board with regard to the unlicensed health care practices.

(d) Subject to the provisions of this chapter, persons in Rhode Island are authorized to practice as unlicensed health care practitioners and receive remuneration for their services.

Rhode Island Board of Mental Health Counselors and Marriage & Family Therapists

Room 104 3 Capitol Hill
Providence, RI 02908-5097
(401) 222-2828
www.health.ri.gov/applications/MentalHealthCounselor.pdf

Section 1.0 Definitions Wherever used in these rules and regulations, the following terms shall be construed as follows:
"The practice of clinical mental health counseling" means the rendering of professional services to individuals, families or groups for monetary compensation. These professional services would include: 1.7.1 Applying the principals, methods and theories of counseling and/or psychotherapeutic techniques to define goals and develop a treatment plan of action aimed toward the prevention, treatment and resolution of social, mental, and emotional dysfunction and intra- or interpersonal disorders in persons diagnosed at intake as nonpsychotic and not presenting medical problems; and 1.7.2 Engaging in psychotherapy of a nonmedical nature utilizing supervision when appropriate and making referrals to other psychiatric, psychological or medical resources when the person is diagnosed as psychotic or presenting a medical problem.
Section 14.0 Exemptions 14.1 No provisions of the Act shall be construed to limit the practice of medicine, osteopathy, psychology, clinical social work, psychiatric nursing, or other recognized business or profession, or to prevent qualified members of other professions from doing work of a nature consistent with their training so long as they do not hold themselves out to the public as a licensed mental health counselor or marriage and family therapist.
14.2.4 is a rabbi, priest, minister, or member of the clergy of any religious denomination or sect when engaging in activities which are within the scope of the performance of his/her regular or specialized ministerial duties and for which no separate charge is made, or when such activities are performed, with or without charge, for or under the auspices or sponsorship, individually or in conjunction with other, of an established and legally 12 recognized church, denomination, or sect, and when the person rendering service remains accountable to the established authority thereof.

South Carolina

South Carolina Massage/Bodywork Panel
Synergy Business Park
Kingstree Building
110 Centerview Dr.
Columbia SC 29210
(803) 896-4588
boardinfo@llr.sc.gov

Title 40 - Professions and Occupations
CHAPTER 30
Massage/Bodywork Practice Act "Massage/bodywork therapy" means the application of a system of structured touch of the superficial tissues of the human body with the hand, foot, arm, or elbow whether or not the structured touch is aided by hydrotherapy, thermal therapy, a massage device, human hands, or the application to the human body of an herbal preparation.

It is further defined by pressure, friction, stroking, rocking, kneading, percussion, or passive active stretching within the normal anatomical range of movement. Complimentary methods including the external application of water, thermal therapy, hydrotherapy, lubricants, and other topical preparations, including but not limited to herbal remedies, body wraps and salt scrubs.

Department of Labor, Licensing and Regulation Board of Examiners for the Licensure of Professional Counselors, Marriage and Family Therapists, and Psycho-Educational Specialists
Synergy Business Park
Kingstree Building
110 Centerview Dr.
Columbia SC 29210
(803) 896-4588
contactcounselor@llr.sc.gov

SECTION 40-75-20. Definitions.

As used in this article:

(16) "Practice of professional counseling" means functioning as a psycho-therapist and may include, but is not limited to, providing individual therapy, family counseling, group therapy, marital counseling, play therapy, couples counseling, chemical abuse or dependency counseling, vocational counseling, school counseling, rehabilitation counseling, intervention, human growth and development counseling, behavioral modification counseling, and hypnotherapy. The practice of professional counseling may include assessment, crisis intervention, guidance and counseling to facilitate normal growth and development, including educational and career development; utilization of functional assessment and counseling for persons requesting assistance in adjustment to a disability or handicapping condition; and consultation and research. The use of specific methods, techniques, or modalities within the practice of licensed professional counseling is restricted to professional counselors appropriately trained in the use of these methods, techniques, or modalities.

South Dakota

South Dakota board of Massage Therapy
PO Box #340, 1351 N. Harrison Ave.
Pierre, SD 57501
Phone: 605-224-1721
Fax: 1-888-425-3032
SDBMT@midwestsolutionssd.com

36-35-1. Definitions. Terms in this chapter mean:
"Massage," the systematic mobilization of the soft tissues of the body through the application of hands or devices for the purposes of therapy, relaxation, or education through means which include:
- *(a) Pressure, friction, stroking, rocking, kneading, percussion, compression, or stretching;*
- *(b) External application of water, heat, cold, lubricants, or other topical agents; or*
- *(c) The use of devices that mimic or enhance actions done by hands;*

Counselors and Marriage and Family Therapist Examiners
P.O. Box 2164
Sioux Falls, SD 57101
605.331.2927
sdbce.msp@midconetwork.com

36-32-1. Definition of terms. Terms as used in this chapter mean:
"Counseling treatment interventions," the application of cognitive, affective, behavioral, and systemic counseling strategies which include principles of development, wellness, and pathology implemented in the context of a professional counseling relationship;

Tennessee

Tennessee Board of Massage Therapy
665 Mainstream Drive, 2nd Floor
Nashville, TN 37243
(615) 253-2111
www.tn.gov/sos/rules

0870-01-.01 DEFINITIONS. *As used in these rules, the following terms and acronyms shall have the following meaning ascribed to them:*
Massage/bodywork/somatic – The manipulation of the soft tissues of the body with the intention of positively affecting the health and well-being of the client.

PUBLIC CHAPTER NO. 254
"Unlicensed individuals who provide direct care and support to persons supported" means the unlicensed individuals, including their unlicensed direct care and support supervisors, who are employed to provide direct care and support to persons supported within the department of intellectual and developmental disabilities ICF/ID homes and facilities or by agencies that are licensed under title 33 and under contract with this department.

GENERAL RULES AND REGULATIONS GOVERNING CHAPTER 1200-10-2 THE PRACTICE OF REFLEXOLOGY October, 2006 (Revised) 2 1200-10-2-.03 NECESSITY OF REGISTRATION. (1) Except as provided in paragraphs (2) and (4), no person shall engage in the practice of reflexology unless such person has registered with the Division of Health Related Boards. (2) This rule shall not apply to: (a) The activities or services of physicians, chiropractors, physical therapists, occupational therapists, athletic trainers, cosmetologists, registered nurses, or members of other professions licensed, certified, or registered by the state who may, on occasion, apply pressure to specific reflex points in the hands and feet in the course of their work; and (b) The activities or services of massage therapists, licensed pursuant to Tennessee Code Annotated, Title 63, Chapter 18, who use reflexology techniques or methods or who advertise reflexology as a service offered to massage therapy clients.

Board of Licensed Professional Counselors,
Licensed Marital and Family Therapists and Licensed Pastoral Therapists
665 Mainstream Drive, 2nd Floor
Nashville, TN 37243
(615) 741-5735

CHAPTER 0450-01 GENERAL RULES GOVERNING PROFESSIONAL COUNSELORS
0450-01-.01 DEFINITIONS. As used in this rule, the terms and acronyms shall have the following meanings ascribed to them.
Practice of counseling as a mental health services provider - the application of mental health and human development principles in order to: (a) facilitate human development and adjustment throughout the life span; (b) prevent, diagnose, and treat mental, emotional or behavioral disorders and associated disorders which interfere with mental health; (c) conduct assessments and diagnoses for the purpose of establishing treatment goals and objectives within the limitations prescribed in T.C.A. § 63-22-150(1); and (d) plan, implement, and evaluate treatment plans using counseling treatment interventions. Counseling treatment interventions shall mean the application of cognitive, affective, behavioral and systemic counseling strategies which include principles of development, wellness, and pathology that reflect a pluralistic society. Nothing in this definition shall be construed to permit the performance of any act which licensed professional counselors designated as mental health service providers are not educated and trained to perform, nor shall it be construed to permit the designation of testing reports as "psychological".

Texas

Massage Therapy Licensing Program
Texas Department of State Health Services
P.O. Box 149347
Austin, Texas 78714-9347 (512) 834-6616
Fax: (512) 834-6677
massage@dshs.state.tx.us
http://www.dshs.state.tx.us/massage

CHAPTER 455. MASSAGE THERAPY

SUBCHAPTER A. GENERAL PROVISIONS

Sec. 455.001. DEFINITIONS. In this chapter:
"Massage therapy" means the manipulation of soft tissue by hand or through a mechanical or electrical apparatus for the purpose of body massage and includes effleurage (stroking), petrissage (kneading), tapotement (percussion), compression, vibration, friction, nerve strokes, and Swedish gymnastics. The terms "massage," "therapeutic massage," "massage technology," "myotherapy," "body massage," "body rub," or any derivation of those terms are synonyms for "massage therapy."

455.004. APPLICABILITY OF CHAPTER. This chapter does not apply to:
(1) a person licensed in this state as a physician, chiropractor, occupational therapist, physical therapist, nurse, cosmetologist, or athletic trainer or as a member of a similar profession subject to state licensing while the person is practicing within the scope of the license;

Sec. 455.151. LICENSE REQUIRED
A person may not for compensation perform or offer to perform any service with a purported health benefit that involves physical contact with a client unless the person:
(1) holds an appropriate license issued under this chapter; or

(2) is licensed or authorized under other law to perform the service.

(d) The department may issue one or more types of licenses not otherwise provided for by this chapter that authorize the license holder to perform a service described by Subsection (c). The department may adopt rules governing a license issued under this subsection.

(According to www.pathfindertohealth.com/ this may be interpreted to mean the Texas Department of State Health Services may issue a license, or licenses, separate from the massage therapy license which would address other modalities such as energy healing therapy.

Texas State Board of Examiners of Professional Counselors
Texas Department of State Health Services
P.O. Box 149347
Austin, Texas 78714-9347
(512) 834-6658
Fax: (512)834-6677
lpc@dshs.state.tx.us
http://www.dshs.state.tx.us/counselor/

Texas State Board of Examiners of Professional Counselors

Tutke 22, Texas Administrative Code, Chapter 681

(7) Counseling-related field--A mental health discipline utilizing human development, psychotherapeutic, and mental health principles including, but not limited to, clinical or counseling psychology, psychiatry, social work, marriage and family therapy, and counseling and guidance. Non-counseling related fields include, but are not limited to, sociology, education, administration, dance therapy and theology.

(17) Recognized religious practitioner--A rabbi, clergyman, or person of similar status who is a member in good standing of and accountable to a denomination, church, sect or religious organization legally recognized under the Internal Revenue Code, 26 U.S.C. §501(c)(3) and other individuals participating with them in pastoral counseling if:

Laws Governing Energy Medicine Practitioners

(A) the counseling activities are within the scope of the performance of their regular or specialized ministerial duties and are performed under the auspices of sponsorship of the legally recognized denomination, church, sect, religious organization or an integrated auxiliary of a church as defined in Federal Tax Regulations, 26 Code of Federal Regulations, §1.6033-2(g)(i) (2012);

(B) the individual providing the service remains accountable to the established authority of that denomination, church, sect, religious organization or integrated auxiliary; and

(C) the person does not use the title of or hold himself or herself out as a professional counselor.

SUBCHAPTER B. AUTHORIZED COUNSELING METHODS AND PRACTICES.

§681.31. Counseling Methods and Practices. The use of specific methods, techniques, or modalities within the practice of professional counseling is limited to professional counselors appropriately trained and competent in the use of such methods, techniques, or modalities. Authorized counseling methods techniques and modalities may include, but are not restricted to, the following:
(11) psychotherapy which utilizes interpersonal, cognitive, cognitive-behavioral, behavioral, psychodynamic, and affective methods and/or strategies to assist clients in their efforts to recover from mental or emotional issues

(13) hypnotherapy which utilizes the principles of hypnosis and post-hypnotic suggestion in the treatment of mental and emotional issues and addictions;
(14) expressive modalities utilized in the treatment of interpersonal, emotional or mental health issues, chemical dependency, or human developmental issues. Modalities include but are not limited to, music, art, dance movement, or the use of techniques employing animals in providing treatment;

Utah

Massage Therapy Licensing Board
160 East 300 South
Salt Lake City, Utah 84111
(801) 530-6628
doplweb@utah.gov
http://www.dopl.utah.gov/licensing/massage_therapy

The Division of Occupational and Professional Licensing and the Massage Therapy Licensing Board have reviewed the practice of Reiki to determine whether Reiki is a modality of massage therapy.
Utah Code Annotated Subsections 58-47b-102(6) and (7) state:
(6) "Practice of massage therapy" means:

 (a) the examination, assessment, and evaluation of the soft tissue of the body for the purpose of devising a treatment plan to promote homeostasis;

 (b) the systematic manual or mechanical manipulation of the soft tissue of the body for the purpose of:

  (i) promoting the therapeutic health and well-being of a client;

  (ii) enhancing the circulation of the blood and lymph;

  (iii) relaxing and lengthening muscles;

  (iv) relieving pain;

  (v) restoring metabolic balance;

  (vi) achieving homeostasis; or

  (vii) other purposes

 (c) the use of the hands or a mechanical or electrical apparatus in connection with this Subsection (6)

 (d) the use of rehabilitative procedures involving the soft tissue of the body ;

 (e) range of motion or movements without spinal adjustment as set forth in Section 58-73-102;

 (f) oil rubs, heat lamps, salt glows, hot and cold packs, or tub, shower, steam, and cabinet baths;

 (g) manual traction and stretching exercise;

 (h) correction of muscular distortion by treatment of the soft tissues of the body;

Laws Governing Energy Medicine Practitioners

(i) counseling, education, and other advisory services to reduce the incidence and severity of physical disability, movement dysfunction, and pain;

(j) similar or related activities and modality techniques; and

(l) providing, offering, or advertising a paid service using the term massage or a derivative of the word massage, regardless of whether the service involves physical conduct.

(7) "Soft tissue" means the muscles and related connective tissue.

Utah Administrative Code Subsection R156-47b-102(8) states:

(8) "Manipulation" as used in Subsection 58-47b-102(6) means contact with movement, involving touching the clothed or unclothed body.

Reiki is defined as a "spiritual healing art" that is performed on an individual by a Reiki Practitioner by "transmitting healing life force energy" through the hands. It is the position of the Division that to the extent that Reiki is used as a "spiritual healing art" and does not involve the methods outlined in the scope of practice of massage therapy, the Reiki is not a modality of massage.

However, should a Reiki Practitioner while performing the a "spiritual healing art" involve the use of any of the methods outlined in the scope of practice of massage therapy, then the Reiki Practitioner must be licensed as a massage therapist.

Nothing is said about other energy healing modalities.

Utah Division of Occupational and Professional Licensing Board
160 East 300 South
Salt Lake City, Utah 84111
(801) 530-6628
doplweb@utah.gov
http://www.dopl.utah.gov/licensing/psychology

R156. Commerce, Occupational and Professional Licensing.
Rule R156-60c. Clinical Mental Health Counselor Licensing Act Rule
As in effect on April 1, 2015

I found no clear cut definition of counseling in the statutes.

Vermont

Vermont does not have a state board of massage therapy.
Some local cities and counties have rules concerning massage. I found nothing concerning energy medicine.

Vermont Board of Allied Mental Health
89 Main Street, 3rd Floor
Montpelier VT 05620-3402
802-828-2390
www.sec.state.vt.us/professional-regulation/profession/allied-mental-health.aspx

Title 26: Professions and Occupations
Chapter 78: Roster Of Psychotherapists Who Are Nonlicensed And Noncertified
"Psychotherapist who is nonlicensed and noncertified" means a person who practices psychotherapy and is neither a licensed psychologist, clinical social worker, or mental health counselor, nor a certified marriage and family therapist or a psychoanalyst.
"Psychotherapy" means the provision of treatment, diagnosis, evaluation, or counseling services to individuals or groups, for a consideration, for the purpose of alleviating mental disorders. "Psychotherapy" involves the application of therapeutic techniques to understand unconscious or conscious motivation, resolve emotional, relationship, or attitudinal conflicts, or modify behavior which interferes with effective emotional, social, or mental functioning. "Psychotherapy" follows a systematic procedure of psychotherapeutic intervention which takes place on a regular basis over a period of time, or, in the case of evaluation and brief psychotherapies, in a single or limited number of interventions. If a person is employed by or under contract with the agency of human services, this definition does not apply to persons with less than a master's degree, to persons providing life skills training or instruction, such as learning to make friends, to handle social situations, to do laundry, and to develop community awareness, or interactions of employees or contracted individuals with clients whose job description or contract specifications do not specifically mention "psychotherapy" as a job responsibility or duty.

Laws Governing Energy Medicine Practitioners

4085. Exemptions

(a) The provisions of this chapter shall not apply to persons while engaged in the course of their customary duties as clergy, licensed physicians, nurses, osteopaths, optometrists, dentists, lawyers, psychologists, social workers, mental health counselors, certified marriage and family therapists, licensed alcohol and drug counselors, and psychoanalysts or licensed educators when performing their duties consistent with the accepted standards of their respective professions.

In the activities and services of the clergy or leader of any religious denomination or sect or a Christian Science practitioner when engaging in activities that are within the scope of the performance of the person's regular or specialized ministerial duties and for which no separate charge is made, or when these activities are performed, with or without charge, for or under the auspices of sponsorship, individually or in conjunction with others, of an established and legally recognizable church, denomination, or sect, and when the person rendering services remains accountable to the established authority of that church, denomination, or sect.

(c) The prohibitions of this chapter shall not apply to practices in the fields of:
- (1) Body work education and healing, including massage therapy, stress reduction, physical fitness, or yoga.
- (2) Energy-related therapy, including kinesiology, crystology, and sound therapy.
- (3) Psychic reading and healing arts, including astrology, channeling, and palmistry.

Virginia

The Virginia Board of Nursing oversees the rules and regulations for massage therapy.

Virginia Department of Health Professions
Virginia Board of Nursing
Perimeter Center
9960 Mayland Drive, Suite 300
Henrico, Virginia 23233-1463 - Directions
Hours: Mon-Fri 8:15 to 5:00 except Holidays
Main Phone: (804) 367-4400

54.1-3000. Definitions.

As used in this chapter, unless the context requires a different meaning:

"Massage therapy" means the treatment of soft tissues for therapeutic purposes by the application of massage and bodywork techniques based on the manipulation or application of pressure to the muscular structure or soft tissues of the human body. The terms "massage therapy" and "therapeutic massage" do not include the diagnosis or treatment of illness or disease or any service or procedure for which a license to practice medicine, nursing, chiropractic therapy, physical therapy, occupational therapy, acupuncture, or podiatry is required by law.

Virginia Board of Counseling
Perimeter Center
9960 Mayland Drive, Suite 300
Henrico Virginia 23233-1463
(804) 367-4610
coun@dhp.virginia.gov

Laws Governing Energy Medicine Practitioners

54.1-3500. Definitions

"Counseling" means the application of principles, standards, and methods of the counseling profession in (i) conducting assessments and diagnoses for the purpose of establishing treatment goals and objectives and (ii) planning, implementing, and evaluating treatment plans using treatment interventions to facilitate human development and to identify and remediate mental, emotional, or behavioral disorders and associated distresses that interfere with mental health.

"Practice of counseling" means rendering or offering to render to individuals, groups, organizations, or the general public any service involving the application of principles, standards, and methods of the counseling profession, which shall include appraisal, counseling, and referral activities.

"Professional counselor" means a person trained in the application of principles, standards, and methods of the counseling profession, including counseling interventions designed to facilitate an individual's achievement of human development goals and remediating mental, emotional, or behavioral disorders and associated distresses that interfere with mental health and development.

Washington

Health Systems Quality Assurance
Town Center 2
111 Israel Road SE
Tumwater WA 98501
360-236-4700
http://www.doh.wa.gov/AboutUs/ProgramsandServices/HealthSystems
QualityAssurance

RCW 18.108.010
Definitions.

"Certified reflexologist" means an individual who is certified under this chapter.

"Massage practitioner" means an individual licensed under this chapter.

"Massage" and *"massage therapy"* mean a health care service involving the external manipulation or pressure of soft tissue for therapeutic purposes. Massage therapy includes techniques such as tapping, compressions, friction, reflexology, Swedish gymnastics or movements, gliding, kneading, shaking, and fascial or connective tissue stretching, with or without the aids of superficial heat, cold, water, lubricants, or salts. Massage therapy does not include diagnosis or attempts to adjust or manipulate any articulations of the body or spine or mobilization of these articulations by the use of a thrusting force, nor does it include genital manipulation.
"Reflexology" means a health care service that is limited to applying alternating pressure with thumb and finger techniques to reflexive areas of the lower one-third of the extremities, feet, hands, and outer ears based on reflex maps. Reflexology does not include the diagnosis of or treatment for specific diseases, or joint manipulations.
18.108.030
Licensure or certification required.

(1)(a) No person may practice or represent himself or herself as a massage practitioner without first applying for and receiving from the department a license to

practice. However, this subsection does not prohibit a certified reflexologist from practicing reflexology.

(b) A person represents himself or herself as a massage practitioner when the person adopts or uses any title or any description of services that incorporates one or more of the following terms or designations: Massage, massage practitioner, massage therapist, massage therapy, therapeutic massage, massage technician, massage technology, massagist, masseur, masseuse, myotherapist or myotherapy, touch therapist, reflexologist except when used by a certified reflexologist, acupressurist, body therapy or body therapist, or any derivation of those terms that implies a massage technique or method.

(2)(a) No person may practice reflexology or represent himself or herself as a reflexologist by use of any title without first being certified as a reflexologist or licensed as a massage practitioner by the department.

(b) A person represents himself or herself as a reflexologist when the person adopts or uses any title in any description of services that incorporates one or more of the following terms or designations: Reflexologist, reflexology, foot pressure therapy, foot reflex therapy, or any derivation of those terms that implies a reflexology technique or method. However, this subsection does not prohibit a licensed massage practitioner from using any of these terms as a description of services.

(c) A person may not use the term "certified reflexologist" without first being certified by the department.

Washington State Department of Health
Town Center 2
111 Israel Road SE
Tumwater WA 98501
360-236-4700
counselorleg@doh.wa.gov.

RCW 18.225.010
Definitions.

The definitions in this section apply throughout this chapter unless the context clearly requires otherwise.

Psychotherapy under the supervision of a licensed independent clinical social worker, psychiatrist, psychologist, psychiatric advanced registered nurse practitioner, psychiatric nurse, or other mental health professionals as may be defined by rules adopted by the secretary;

"Mental health counseling" means the application of principles of human development, learning theory, psychotherapy, group dynamics, and etiology of mental illness and dysfunctional behavior to individuals, couples, families, groups, and organizations, for the purpose of treatment of mental disorders and promoting optimal mental health and functionality. Mental health counseling also includes, but is not limited to, the assessment, diagnosis, and treatment of mental and emotional disorders, as well as the application of a wellness model of mental health

RCW 18.83.010
Definitions.
When used in this chapter

(1) The "practice of psychology" means the observation, evaluation, interpretation, and modification of human behavior by the application of psychological principles, methods, and procedures for the purposes of preventing or eliminating symptomatic or maladaptive behavior and promoting mental and behavioral health. It includes, but is not limited to, providing the following services to individuals, families, groups, organizations, and the public, whether or not payment is received for services rendered:

(a) Psychological measurement, assessment, and evaluation by means of psychological, neuropsychological, and psychoeducational testing;

(b) Diagnosis and treatment of mental, emotional, and behavioral disorders, and psychological aspects of illness, injury, and disability; and

(c) Counseling and guidance, psychotherapeutic techniques, remediation, health promotion, and consultation within the context of established psychological principles and theories.

This definition does not include the teaching of principles of psychology for accredited educational institutions, or the conduct of research in problems of human or animal behavior.

RCW 18.19.020
Definitions.
The definitions in this section apply throughout this chapter unless the context clearly requires otherwise.
"Counseling" means employing any therapeutic techniques, including but not limited to social work, mental health counseling, marriage and family therapy, and hypnotherapy, for a fee that offer, assist or attempt to assist an individual or individuals in the amelioration or adjustment of mental, emotional, or behavioral problems, and includes therapeutic techniques to achieve sensitivity and awareness of self and others and the development of human potential. For the purposes of this chapter, nothing may be construed to imply that the practice of hypnotherapy is necessarily limited to counseling.
"Counselor" means an individual, practitioner, therapist, or analyst who engages in the practice of counseling to the public for a fee, including for the purposes of this chapter, hypnotherapists.
"Hypnotherapist" means a person registered under this chapter who is practicing hypnosis as a modality.
"Psychotherapy" means the practice of counseling using diagnosis of mental disorders according to the fourth edition of the diagnostic and statistical manual of mental disorders, published in 1994, and the development of treatment plans for counseling based on diagnosis of mental disorders in accordance with established practice standards.

West Virginia

West Virginia Massage Therapy Licensure Board
Peoples Building, 179 Summers St Suite 711
Charleston, WV 25301
(304) 558-1060
http://www.wvmassage.org/rules.asp

ARTICLE 37. MASSAGE THERAPISTS.
§30-37-2. Definitions.
"Massage therapist" means a person licensed to practice the health care service of massage therapy under this article who practices or administers massage therapy to a client of either gender for compensation. No person licensed by the massage therapy licensure board may be referred to as a primary care provider nor be permitted to use such designation.
"Massage therapy" means a health care service which is a scientific and skillful manipulation of soft tissue for therapeutic or remedial purposes, specifically for improving muscle tone, circulation, promoting health and physical well-being. Massage therapy includes massage, myotherapy, massotherapy, bodywork, bodywork therapy, or therapeutic massage including hydrotherapy, superficial hot and cold applications, vibration and topical applications or other therapies which involve manipulation of the muscle and connective tissue of the body, for the purpose of enhancing health, reducing stress, improving circulation, aiding muscle relaxation, increasing range of motion, or relieving neuro-muscular pain. Massage therapy does not include diagnosis or service which requires a license to practice medicine or surgery, osteopathic medicine, chiropractic, or podiatry, and does not include service performed by nurses, occupational therapists, or physical therapists who act under their own professional license, certificate or registration.
30-37-11. Exemptions.
Nothing in this article may be construed to prohibit or otherwise limit:
(a) The practice of a profession by persons who are licensed, certified or registered under the laws of this state and who are performing services within their authorized scope of practice. Persons exempted under this subdivision include, but are

not limited to, those licensed, certified or registered to practice within the scope of any branch of medicine, nursing, osteopathy, chiropractic and podiatry, as well as licensed, certified or registered barbers, cosmetologists, athletic trainers, physical and occupational therapists; and any student enrolled in a program of massage education at a school approved by the West Virginia State College System Board or by a state agency in another state, the District of Columbia or a United States territory which approves educational programs and which meets qualifications for the National Certification Exam administered through the National Certification Board for Therapeutic Massage and Bodywork, provided that the student does not hold himself or herself out as a licensed massage therapist and does not charge or receive a fee

West Virginia Board of Examiners in Counseling
815 Quarrier Street, Suite 212
Charleston, West Virginia 25301
(800) 520-3852
rclay27@msn.com
http://www.wvbec.org/allaboutwvbec

30-31-3. *Definitions*
As used in this article, the following words and terms have the following meanings, unless the context clearly indicates otherwise:
"Clinical counseling procedures" means an approach to counseling that emphasizes the counselor's role in systematically assisting clients through all the following including, but not limited to, observing, assessing, and analyzing background and current information; utilizing assessment techniques useful in appraising aptitudes, abilities, achievements, interests or attitudes; diagnosing and developing a treatment plan. The goal of these procedures is the prevention or elimination of symptomatic, maladaptive, or undesired behavior, cognitions, or emotions in order to integrate a wellness, preventative, pathology and multicultural model of human behavior to assist an individual, couple, family, group of individuals, organization, institution or community to achieve mental, emotional, physical, social, moral, educational, spiritual, vocational or career development and adjustment

through the life span of the individual, couple, family, group of individuals, organization, institution or community.

"Professional counseling" means the assessment, diagnosis, treatment and prevention of mental, emotional or addiction disorders through the application of clinical counseling procedures. Professional counseling includes the use of psychotherapy, assessment instruments, counseling, consultation, treatment planning, and supervision in the delivery of services to individuals, couples, families and groups.

30-31-11. Persons exempted from licensure
The following activities are exempt from the provisions of this article:
The activities and services of qualified members of other recognized professions such as physicians, psychologists, pyschoanalysts, social workers, lawyers, clergy, nurses or teachers performing counseling or marriage and family therapy consistent with the laws of this state, their training and any code of ethics of their professions as long as such person do not represent themselves as licensed professional counselors or licensed marriage and family therapists as defined by section three of this article.

Wisconsin

Department of Safety and Professional Services
Massage Therapy and Bodywork Affiliated Credentialing Board
55 N Dickinson St
Madison, WI 53703
(608) 266-2112
http://dsps.wi.gov/LicensesPermitsRegistrations/Credentialing-Division-Home-Page/Health-Professions/Massage-Therapist-or-Bodywork-Therapist

MTBT 1.02 Definitions. As used in chs. MTBT 1 to 7, unless the context otherwise requires:
"Massage therapy or bodywork therapy" means the science and healing art that uses manual actions and adjunctive therapies to palpate and manipulate the soft tissue of the human body, in order to improve circulation, reduce tension, relieve soft tissue pain, or increase flexibility. Massage therapy or bodywork therapy includes determining whether manual actions and adjunctive therapies are appropriate. Massage therapy or bodywork therapy does not include making a medical, physical therapy, or chiropractic diagnosis.

Marriage & Family Therapy, Professional Counseling & Social Work
Department of Safety and Professional Services
1400 East Washington Avenue, Room 112
Madison, WI 53703
608) 266-2112
dsps@wisconsin.gov
http://dsps.wi.gov/

MPSW 1.02 Definitions

"Psychotherapy" means the diagnosis and treatment of mental, emotional, or behavioral disorders, conditions, or addictions through the application of methods derived from established psychological or systemic principles for the purpose of assisting people in modifying their behaviors, cognitions, emotions, and other personal characteristics, which may include the purpose of understanding unconscious processes or intrapersonal, interpersonal, or psychosocial dynamics

Laws Governing Energy Medicine Practitioners

Wyoming

Wyoming does not have a massage board at the time of this writing. I found this under physical therapy. It mentions massage, but nothing about energy work.

CHAPTER 25 - PHYSICAL THERAPISTS

33-25-101. Definitions.

(a) As used in this act:

(i) "Physical therapy" or "physiotherapy" means the care and services provided by or under the direction and supervision of a physical therapist or physiotherapist who is licensed pursuant to this act. The practice of physical therapy includes:

(A) Examining, evaluating and testing persons with mechanical, physiological or developmental impairments, functional limitations, disabilities or other health or movement related conditions to determine a physical therapy diagnosis, prognosis or plan of treatment and assessing the ongoing effects of intervention;

(B) Alleviating impairments, functional limitations or disabilities by designing, implementing or modifying treatment interventions that may include but are not limited to:

(I) Therapeutic exercise;

(II) Functional activities in the home;

(III) Community or work integration or reintegration;

(IV) Manual therapy, which includes mobilization and grades I through IV manipulation of joints and soft tissue but does not include grade V

manipulations without completion of advanced training requirements as determined by the board;

    (V) Therapeutic massage;

Wyoming State Mental Health Professions Licensing Board
Wyoming State Board of Psychology
2001 Capitol Ave RM 104
Cheyenne, WY 82002
(307) 777-3628
WyoMHPLB@wyo.gov

"Practice of psychology" means the observation, description, evaluation, interpretation and modification of human behavior by the application of psychological principles, methods and procedures, for the purpose of any one (1) or any combination of the following:
    (A) Preventing, eliminating, evaluating or assessing symptomatic, maladaptive or undesired behavior;
    (B) Enhancing interpersonal relationships, work and life adjustment, personal effectiveness, behavioral health and mental health;
    (E) Psychoanalysis, psychotherapy, hypnosis, biofeedback and behavior analysis and therapy;

33-27-114. Exemptions.

(a) Nothing in this act shall be construed to prevent members of other recognized professions who are licensed, certified or regulated under the laws of this state as defined in the rules and regulations from rendering services consistent with their professional training and code of ethics, provided that they do not represent themselves to be psychologists.

(c) Duly recognized members of the clergy shall not be restricted from functioning in their ministerial capacity, provided they do not represent themselves to be psychologists.

Laws across Canada

In Canada there are a number of levels of government just as there are in the United States. Generally each province is responsible for health care. The federal government is responsible for products. In terms of integrative therapy, or in terms of herbal products, or pharmaceuticals or things like that, the federal government is usually responsible, just like the Food and Drug Administration carries responsibility in the United States.

Health Canada has branches that regulate pharmaceuticals, vitamin products, and other healthcare products. They determine whether such products can be sold in Canada.

If a practitioner wanted to sell something that was ingestable, they would have to check with Health Canada to find the regulations for that product. Nutritional supplements that make any claims whatsoever, would come under federal regulations in terms of being cleared for sale in Canada. You must go through channels if you want to bring a product into the country. If it has not been approved, you may not bring it into the country with the intention to sell it as part of your practice.

Labelling is a big issue as well. The rules are somewhat similar to the United States. However, even though a product has passed scrutiny in the United States, it may not be acceptable for sale in Canada.

A lot of products are confiscated at the border, even from Canadians who bought the product in the United States. That can go both ways. Products approved in Canada might not be approved in the states.

Anything to do with mind/body regulations or anything that involves touch does not have any national or provincial regulations in Canada. If someone is practicing psychotherapy without a license, or practicing nursing without a license, etc. then those regulatory bodies would step in and prevent the person from continuing that work.

Each province has regulatory bodies for their physicians, massage therapists, nurses, psychotherapists, etc.

However, local cities may have specific regulations concerning touch and/or energy work. For example, Toronto, a number of years ago passed legislation requiring people to have a massage license in order to practice within the city. They were trying to prevent illegal masseuse and prostitution from hiding behind the guise of body work. So in order to touch in any way in Toronto, you must have a license.

To find out what the regulations are in your town, contact city hall and ask for the licensing department. They will tell you what you need to know.

Nurses who practice Healing Touch, or any other form of energy therapy, need to check with their college or regulatory body to determine if they can use their credentials as an RN with their name as an energy medicine practitioner.

There are provinces in Canadian, specifically Saskatchewan and possibly Alberta, that will not allow nurses who have certification in an energy medicine discipline, such as Therapeutic Touch, to put RN with their name when they are advertising their energy medicine practice. This may also be true for doctors and other healthcare professionals. It is best to check.

Practitioners in Canada are encouraged to obtain a waver from their local or city government stating their practice is legal and doesn't involve illegal massage parlor activities or prostitution. It's not required, but is definitely a good idea, especially if someone is questioning your work.

Be sure to check with your local authorities concerning psychotherapy laws as well. Some energy medicine practices, such as the ones involving tapping, may be of concern by the agencies regulating psychotherapy. Counseling of any kind has its own regulations.

Most of the well known disciplines in energy medicine, such as Healing Touch, Therapeutic Touch, Reiki, etc. are known to the city authorities who regulate forms of touch. However, if you are using a discipline unknown to them you may have to present a case to allow the practice of that discipline.

Canadian Examining Board of Health Care Practitioners, Inc
658 Danforth Ave. Suite 204
Toronto, Ontario M4J 5B9
(416) 466-9755
Celebinc@rogers.com
http://canadianexaminingboard.com/

The Canadian Examining Board of Health Care Practitioners, Inc. is a private not-for-profit, federally chartered organization which promotes health care programs of Complementary Medicines. This progressive body has set standards of professional qualifications for health care practitioners in this field, and provides a forum for the development, exchange, and dissemination of knowledge and skills appropriate to the requirements of professional complementary health care practice. Having established a code of ethics, conduct, and practice, the Canadian Examining board recognizes institutions which meet their stringent standards and offers legal designations for professional health care practitioners who have graduated from these approved programs.

The Canadian Examining Board of Health Care Practitioners, a certified educational institution by the minister of Human Resources under Sections 118.5 and 118.6 of the Income Tax Act, is a complementary health care organization which has, since 1991, set professional and measurable working standards for the field of complementary health care. This has been done in order to promote and support effective, safe, and ethical holistic health care practices. In order to receive Board designations – recognized by the Holistic Practitioners Business Bylaw of Toronto and federally recognized across Canada – practitioners must have graduated from one of our twenty-seven approved institutions which teach complementary health care programs that meet our astringent professional standards.
http://www.toronto.ca/legdocs/2005/agendas/committees/plt/plt051107/it011.pdf

Made in the USA
Middletown, DE
04 February 2019